Don't Just Sit There!

*The challenge to get up and
do what Jesus would do*

Jack McKee

AMBASSADOR INTERNATIONAL
Greenville, South Carolina • Belfast, Northern Ireland

Don't Just Sit There!
© Copyright 2008 Jack McKee

All Bible references are taken from the NIV unless otherwise stated.

*Adm. by worshiptogether.com songs
excl. UK & Europe, adm. by
kingsway songs.com
tym@kingsway.co.uk

ISBN 978-1-84030-200-4

Ambassador Publications
a division of
Ambassador Productions Ltd.
Providence House
Ardenlee Street,
Belfast,
BT6 8QJ
Northern Ireland
www.ambassador-productions.com

Emerald House
427 Wade Hampton Blvd.
Greenville
SC 29609, USA
www.emeraldhouse.com

Don't Just Sit There!

Dedication

The book is dedicated to all true believers who 'Don't just sit there', but who live and walk as true Ambassadors of Christ.

This book is also dedicated to the memory of Linda Martin, who was Pastor Jack's secretary, but who sadly died in tragic circumstances. Linda is mentioned in Chapter 9 as one who travelled to Albania in an act of kindness in a team led by Pastor Jack's wife, Kathleen.

"We are therefore Christ's ambassadors, as though God were making his appeal through us" (2 Cor. 5:20).

About the Author

Pastor Jack McKee has become somewhat of an enigma to many of his contemporaries, both within the church and within the community he seeks to serve and reach with the Gospel of Jesus Christ.

Having been greatly challenged by the life of David Wilkerson, founder of Teen Challenge, Jack recognised that true followers of Christ 'Don't just sit there', instead they get up and step up and become active on the battlefields of life as 'Ambassadors of Christ', which is the core theme of this book.

Leaving military service in Northern Ireland, where he had served as a member of the Ulster Defence Regiment (UDR) for five years, and having avoided death several times when some of his friends and comrades were tragically murdered by terrorists, he chose to give up the gun for the greater cause of taking up the cross.

In 1977 he left Northern Ireland to study at the Elim Bible College in England. After graduating in 1979, he was accepted as a probationary minister and was finally ordained as an Elim minister in 1982. Jack had attended Bible College with the belief that God was calling him far beyond the safety of a church platform. Instead Jack's pastorate would be the dangerous streets and alleyways of his war torn community, the notorious Shankill Road.

A more detailed account of his dramatic story of life and ministry in strife-torn Northern Ireland has been documented in his first book 'Through Terror and Adversity', published by Alpha Publications and distributed by Kingsway Publications, Eason's and World Books. This can also be ordered on the New Life City Church web site at www.newlifecitychurch.co.uk.

In Pastor Jack's second book 'The Cross and the Gun', he tells of his amazing journey in following through the commitment he had made as a Shankill Road teenager to Jesus Christ. This journey has not only taken him across the world, but more specifically from the streets of Belfast to a Bible college in the South of England and eventually back again to Belfast, where his ministry has taken a leap beyond the norm.

In his second book you will read of his walk through the centre of his own community while carrying a cross during a bloody feud between the UVF and the UDA/UFF Loyalist Paramilitaries when many lost their lives and when many more were seriously wounded. You will also read of his incredible and daring 40 Day Cross Walk through the divided and warring communities of the Catholic Falls Road and the neighbouring Protestant Shankill Road in West Belfast.

Finally, you will read of his congregation's courageous faith-response to a bloody and deadly feud within the ranks of the UDA/UFF that seriously affected the Lower Shankill, and more specifically the surrounding streets where his church, New Life City Church, is located and where many of the families that attend his church actually live.

Contents

1. Ambassadors of Christ 11
2. Ambassadors of Reconciliation 15
3. Ambassadors of Influence .25
4. Ambassadors of Character 37
5. Ambassadors of Christian Love 47
6. Ambassadors of Christian Joy 55
7. Ambassadors of Peace 67
8. Ambassadors of Patience .79
9. Ambassadors of Kindness .89
10. Ambassadors of Goodness 97
11. Ambassadors of Faithfulness 103
12. Ambassadors of Gentleness 111
13. Ambassadors of Self-Control 119
14. Ambassadors of The Anointing 127
15. Ambassadors of Authority 137
16. Ambassadors of Power 151
17. Ambassadors of the Cross 163

1

Ambassadors of Christ

*Therefore, if anyone is in Christ, he is a new creation;
the old has gone, the new has come! All this is from
God, who reconciled us to himself through Christ and
gave us the ministry of reconciliation: that God was
reconciling the world to himself in Christ, not
counting men's sins against them. And he has
committed to us the message of reconciliation. We are
therefore Christ's ambassadors, as though God were
making his appeal through us. We implore you on
Christ's behalf: Be reconciled to God (2Cor.5:17-20).*

As teenagers, Kathleen and I lived just a few doors apart. We'd
grown up in the same tough environment of Belfast, Northern
Ireland. Our young lives were destined to come together for a
purpose far greater than anything our sometimes mischievous

minds could have imagined. However, having separately committed our lives to Christ in 1966 and 1967 respectively, Kathleen and I soon connected with each other and began a relationship that would not only last to this present day, but one that would experience the kind of pressures that had the potential of destroying our relationship, our marriage, and even our lives.

However, those same pressures have not only served to strengthen our relationship, but have built within us the kind of character and determination that has enabled us to resist the temptation to quit and join the ranks of the spiritual couch potato. Those same pressures that were meant to destroy us, God used for our good. Those same pressures that were sent with an evil intent to weaken and to break us were turned around by the transforming power of the Spirit of God so that they had the opposite effect.

Little did we know, as teenagers in love, that we were not only being called to follow Christ, but we were also being called to represent Him in a land once visited by 'Saint' Patrick, whose message was one of love and forgiveness. Yet the land he visited has since been stained with the blood of many of its children, slain not so much by the stranger from without, but slain by those who were born and who lived on the same harmless looking island that sits on the eastern edge of a raging Atlantic ocean.

We were being called to serve in a land, known affectionately as the Emerald Isle because of its lush arable fields. From the air it looks like a patterned hand-woven grassy quilt with forty different shades of green, where every river is fringed by grassy slopes, and where its mountains sweep down to the sea.

Now believe me, I do not want to appear to be bragging or to be name dropping. However, due to the ambassadorial nature of this book, I think it is appropriate to mention that I have had the privilege to meet and dine with two Ambassadors. These were the Irish Ambassador to the USA in Washington DC and the American Ambassador to Ireland (Jean Kennedy Smith, sister of the late John F Kennedy); whom I met for a second time in Belfast while writing this book. Besides these, I have met with several US Consul Generals in Belfast who represent the US Ambassador to the United Kingdom.

What is an Ambassador?

An ambassador is described as a high ranking diplomatic official. He or she is someone who is sent by one sovereign to another or by one country to another as its resident representative. An ambassador is someone who belongs to one country, yet lives in another, and is given special ambassadorial and diplomatic rights. As long as they continue to live in the host country as an ambassador, they represent the higher power that sent them, e.g. a king. However, they represent the king in such a way it is as if the king himself is in residence in the host country, so much so that to receive the ambassador is to receive the king who sent him. To reject the ambassador is to reject the king he represents, and to insult the ambassador is equal to insulting his king.

In the Old Testament book of 2 Samuel we read, "In the course of time, the king of the Ammonites died, and his son Hanun succeeded him as king. David thought, "I will show kindness to Hanun son of Nahash, just as his father showed kindness to me." So David sent a delegation to express his sympathy to Hanun concerning his father. When David's men came to the land of the Ammonites, the Ammonite nobles said to Hanun their lord, "Do you think David is honouring your father by sending men to you to express sympathy? Hasn't David sent them to you to explore the city and spy it out and overthrow it?" So Hanun seized David's men, shaved off half of each man's beard, cut off their garments in the middle at the buttocks, and sent them away. When David was told about this, he sent messengers to meet the men, for they were greatly humiliated. The king said, "Stay at Jericho till your beards have grown, and then come back." (2 Sam.10:1-5). We are then told in verse 6 that the Ammonites became a stench in David's nostrils; but why? Because to insult the ambassador, was tantamount to insulting the King.

With the above in mind, let me remind you that Paul said, "We are therefore Christ's ambassadors, as though God were making his appeal through us" (2 Cor.10:20). We so represent Christ as his Ambassadors that anything done to us equates to being done to Christ. This is why Jesus said, "He who receives you receives me, and he who receives me receives the one who sent me." (Matt. 10:40).

It is also why Jesus said, "Whatever you did for one of the least of these brothers of mine, you did for me." (Matt. 25:40). It is for this same reason the church is spoken of as the Body of Christ, because we so represent Christ on this earth it is as though he is still resident on the earth through us.

We therefore, as Christians, are his Ambassadors. For this reason everything we do, we do in his name; we do in his power; we do with his authority and we do with his protection. That is why Jesus said, "All authority in heaven and on earth has been given to me. Therefore go and make disciples of all nations, baptizing them in the name of the Father and of the Son and of the Holy Spirit, and teaching them to obey everything I have commanded you. And surely I am with you always, to the very end of the age" (Matt.28: 18-20).

It was with this compelling sense of commission that Kathleen and I set off on an incredible journey together. We did so with the belief and hope that in some small way we could impact our world by being a God-influence first of all to our city and then beyond as ambassadors of Christ. We did so not knowing where the journey would lead, but knowing that Christ would be with us every step of the way and in every situation. We did so because we were not content to just sit there.

2

Ambassadors of Reconciliation

"God.....gave us the ministry of reconciliation"
(2. Cor.5:18)

If you were to read again the verses in 2 Cor.5:17-20 you will find that Paul has provided several clues that point us in the right direction regarding the first responsibility of an ambassador of Christ. These clues are as follows: that God has "reconciled us to himself"; that he has given us the "ministry of reconciliation"; that he was "reconciling the world to himself"; that he has committed to us the "ministry of reconciliation"; and that we are called to "be reconciled to God".

How clear is this? For here we see that five times Paul mentions reconciliation (reconciling, reconciled), not only as something that God desires to achieve, but as something that God desires his ambassadors to actively participate in as a ministry. I want to therefore show from the outset that first and foremost ambassadors of Christ are ambassadors of reconciliation.

Reconciled to God

Ambassadors of Christ are those who must first of all have been reconciled to God through Christ. It would not be possible for anyone to be an ambassador of reconciliation, in the Biblical sense, unless they first of all have been reconciled to God through Christ and secondly to each other. Yet that is exactly what happened to those of us who are Christians. The moment we came to Christ was the moment we received him and was also the moment we were received by him. The moment we repented of our sins was the very moment we were forgiven for those sins. The moment we received Christ was the same moment that God received us through Christ, and was therefore the very moment that we were reconciled to God.

But how was all of this made possible? It was made possible only through the cross, i.e. our reconciliation to the Father was only made possible through the death of his son Jesus Christ upon the cross. For this was the means by which "God was reconciling the world to himself in Christ" (2 Cor.5:19), and he did so while we were yet his enemies, as Paul said, "When we were God's enemies, we were reconciled to him through the death of his Son" (Rom. 5:10). You see reconciliation only needs to take place between those who are enemies. Friends do not need to be reconciled, unless of course they fall out; husbands and wives do not need to be reconciled, unless they fall out; families do not need to be reconciled, unless there is a falling out within the family. It is only when relationships breakdown, and when people become estranged from each other, that reconciliation is required.

However, enemies always need to be reconciled, and the Bible makes it clear that we, that is, all of us, were enemies of God, and were estranged from God because of our own personal sin. Again I remind you that Paul said, "When we were God's enemies, we were reconciled to him through the death of his Son" (Rom. 5:10). This is why we can draw near to God, as encouraged by Paul when he said, "Let us draw near to God with a sincere heart in full assurance of faith, having our hearts sprinkled to cleanse us from a guilty conscience and having our bodies washed with pure water" (Heb. 10:22). The fact is as committed Christians we have been reconciled to God, but only through the life of Christ and by his efficacious and 'substitutionery' death on the cross.

The ministry of reconciliation

Having explained that the first thing we need to understand is the fact that we have been reconciled to God, it is important to explain that the second thing we need to take hold of is the fact God has given us the ministry of reconciliation. It was for this reason Jesus said, "Follow me and I will make you fishers of men" (Matt 4:19). It was not just follow me, and let's go take a seat somewhere! But in following Jesus we are to actively become involved in reaching others in the hope that they also will follow him.

He has called us to be fishers of men, because he did not intend to stop with us, whether within our families, our schools, our places of employment, or our neighbourhood etc. The fact is God also wants to be reconciled to our loved ones, our school friends, our work mates, and our neighbours etc, but he has chosen to make his appeal through us.

When Jesus spoke to the woman at the well she immediately returned to her home town of Sychar and said to her people, "Come, see a man who told me everything I ever did. Could this be the Christ?" (John 4:29). As a result of this we are told, "They came out of the town and made their way toward him" (John 4:30) and that "Many of the Samaritans from that town believed in him because of the woman's testimony" (John 4:39). You see the meeting that Jesus had with this woman was not just about her, but was also about her family, her friends, neighbours and townspeople.

When the jailer came to faith in Christ (Acts 16), Paul declared that this move of God would not finish with him, but that his household would also come to faith in Christ, because what happened in the prison that night was not just about the jailer, it was also about his family and those in his employment.

When Andrew first met Jesus and believed him to be the Messiah, the Christ, he immediately went looking for his brother Simon Peter and said, "We have found the Messiah", and he brought Peter to Jesus (see John 1:41, 42). When Philip began to follow Jesus he went and found Nathaniel and said, "We have found the one Moses wrote about in the Law, and about whom the prophets also wrote" (John 1:45).

Could you imagine what would have happened had the woman decided to simply sit down at the well where she met Jesus and never wanted to leave that place? What about the people in Sychar? And what if the jailer had just sat there with Paul and Silas in the prison cell where he came to faith in Christ? What about his family and those in his employment? And what if Andrew had never gone for Peter or if Philip had never gone for Nathaniel? What if they had decided to just sit there?

God has therefore called us, not to sit there – somewhere, whether on a pew or on a padded seat, whether in a community centre or in a cathedral. He has not called us to take a seat in a church building on a Sunday, but to take our place in the Kingdom of God and in society as his appointed ambassadors; ambassadors of reconciliation. Along with this appointment he has given us the ministry of reconciliation and the message of reconciliation. The ministry is the calling that God has given to each of us as followers of Christ, whereas the message is the Word of God. The fact is God has not only called us, but has equipped us, and has sent us out as his ambassadors to do as he would do, and to say as he would say, "as if God were making his appeal through us".

However, we are called first and foremost to be reconciled to God, so that having been reconciled we can therefore call upon others to be likewise reconciled to God. This is what Paul was referring to when he said, "We are therefore Christ's ambassadors, as though God were making his appeal through us. We implore you on Christ's behalf: Be reconciled to God" (2 Cor.5:20).

But beyond being reconciled to God, we are also called to be reconciled to each other; that is to each other within the Church and also with those outside the Church. This is also why Jesus said, "First go and be reconciled to your brother; then come and offer your gift" (Matt. 5:24), and then we are told by Paul, "As far as it depends on you, live at peace with everyone" (Rom. 12:18). This does not mean that our role is a passive one where each of us develop a mindset that says, "As long as everyone leaves me alone, I will leave them alone". No, but we are called to actively pursue reconciliation and to encourage it however and whenever possible.

Historically, Northern Ireland has been a country divided by sectarianism along the lines of religion, nationality and culture. Yet it is this division that has provided many opportunities for reconciliation, and we thank God for giving us, as pastors and as an outreach ministry, the wisdom and the ability to reach across the divide and to bring about genuine and lasting reconciliation between people who have been long term traditional enemies. We have been achieving this through our cross-community programmes and through the evangelistic outreach of New Life City Church.

We have witnessed people on opposite sides of Northern Ireland's conflict and on opposing sides of internal feuds being literally reconciled to each other, because they have been reconciled to God through Christ. I sat recently with someone

who at one time was an active member of the IRA and had
served time in prison as a 'lifer' for the murder of a colleague of
mine (although unknown to me personally). There we sat
drinking coffee and looking into each other's eyes. He
commented, "Jack, this is so amazing and can only be God,
because there was a time when I would have gladly killed you
and when you would have killed me if you'd had the chance, but
here we are today, no longer enemies, but brothers in Christ".
This is reconciliation indeed!

Shane Lynch, Boyzone

It was Thursday 3 July, 2008 when almost 500 people gathered
for our first event of its kind in our 'new building', which at the
time of writing is still nothing but an empty warehouse. Yet it
was amazingly transformed to look like a major concert facility
to host our special guest Shane Lynch, a member of Boyzone,
one of the world's most successful Boy Bands from Dublin,
Ireland.

What added to the excitement and to the uniqueness of this
event is the fact that the building is positioned literally on the
dividing line between two opposing and warring communities,
Protestant Shankill and Catholic Falls. These communities have
inflicted so much pain and death on each other that hatred and
suspicion run deep. As a church we have often found ourselves
on the frontline, but this event put us right on the dividing line
with people from both sides of the wall coming together to hear
Shane Lynch speak about his conversion to Christ.

The event began with our New Life Worship Team leading
an awesome time of praise and worship. They looked so good
and sounded like a top team that a man sitting next to me, who
used to work for the BBC, turned and asked, 'Where did you
get the band from, Jack?' He was stunned when I told him it was
our very own Worship Team and that I had taught them

everything I knew about singing and worship! We now need to pray for a little team humility! The worship was followed by Steve Legg, who after having some fun with the audience, interviewed Shane Lynch. During the interview Shane shared his story and his testimony in a truly God-honouring and Christ-uplifting manner. The message of his personal conversion to Christ was so clear, as was the challenge to others to likewise follow Christ.

Immediately after Shane had finished sharing his story our New Life Drama Team took to the platform and did an awesome piece of drama called 'Everything' by Lifehouse. This was followed with an appeal to those who wanted to commit their lives to Christ. Several people responded by raising their hands, with a number coming to the front for prayer and literature. Afterwards there was rejoicing with tears as friends and family members embraced those who had committed their lives to Christ.

The media was there in force with two of Northern Ireland's main newspapers carrying the story the following day. Even before the event was finished it was being shown on both of the main television networks in Northern Ireland (BBC and UTV) and was again repeated during prime time viewing by UTV the following day.

Because the building is situated right on the dividing line between the Shankill and Falls communities, and because it has a security gate attached to the side of the building stretching across the main road, which is closed early every night, we asked for a police presence. They agreed to be on hand, but maintained a low profile as they kept a watchful eye on the security gate that remained open for the event so that people from both sides could gain access. This is the first time that something like this has ever happened. The police said they would close the gate at 9.30 pm, yet they kept it open until almost 10.30 pm. Some of the officers came into the building to purchase Shane Lynch's book 'The Chancer'. They got it autographed and got their photographs taken alongside him to the applause of the crowd.

As ambassadors of reconciliation this was the latest in a series of events aimed at breaking down barriers between two peaceline communities. It is all well and good to see a form of reconciliation between our political parties, but reconciliation between our divided communities is just as important if not more so. The above event was not about reconciling Protestantism and Catholicism. It was not even about religion, but about an act of unity in personal faith and commitment to Jesus Christ. For only then can the walls of division be truly broken down.

Blessed are the peacemakers

I will say more about peacemakers in chapter 7, but for now Jesus said, "Blessed are the peacemakers for they will be called the sons of God" (Matt. 5:9). He does not say blessed are the peace keepers; because it is one thing to be a peace keeper, but a different thing entirely to be a peace-maker. In fact it is much easier to be a peacekeeper by simply remaining passive, but to be a peace-maker you need to become active, even to the point of taking serious risks, and sometimes taking risks that are life threatening.

In fact there are some places in this world where peacemakers will be viewed as peace breakers and as trouble makers, not because they are, but because they are revolutionary enough to go against the grain. Jesus was called a man of peace. In fact one of his messianic titles is Prince of Peace, yet the religious and the political authorities in Israel, including some who represented Rome, viewed him as one of the local rabble rousers and trouble makers.

The fact is, reconcilers are peace-makers; not passive in the sense of being inactive, but actively pursuing peace, which sometimes means speaking out against and working against those negative influences that seek to destroy peace. When it comes to reconciliation, the church should be the first to step up and give a lead, and show a willingness to embrace those who are different, without discrimination or regard of colour, creed or lifestyle, for "There is neither Jew nor Greek, slave nor free, male nor female, for you are all one in Christ Jesus" (Gal. 3:8).

3

Ambassadors of Influence

Jesus said, "You are the salt of the earth. But if the salt loses its saltiness, how can it be made salty again? It is no longer good for anything, except to be thrown out and trampled by men. You are the light of the world. A city on a hill cannot be hidden. Neither do people light a lamp and put it under a bowl. Instead they put it on its stand, and it gives light to everyone in the house. In the same way, let your light shine before men, that they may see your good deeds and praise your Father in heaven" (Matt.5:13-16).

Jesus had just finished his teaching on the 'Beatitudes', which for us, both as Christians and Ambassadors of Christ are the 'Best Attitudes' we can have. When Jesus had finished his teaching, he immediately encouraged his followers to be ambassadors of influence by being salt and light in the earth.

Our Responsibility

It is important to take note of exactly what it was that Jesus said. He said, "*You* are the salt of the earth, and *you* are the light of the world". He did not say those who are Pharisees, or those who are bishops, or those who are priests, or those who are pastors, but he said *you* are salt and *you* are light. He was speaking to those who followed him at that time and to all who would follow him later. He was speaking of the fact that all believers would be God-influencers in a dark and needy world by being salt and light.

Similarly Peter said, "You are a chosen people, a royal priesthood, a holy nation, a people belonging to God, that you may declare the praises of him who called you out of darkness into his wonderful light" (1 Pet 2:9). He then goes on to challenge us to live such good lives that others will glorify God because of what they see in us. "That, though they accuse you of doing wrong, they may see your good deeds and glorify God on the day he visits us" (1 Pet 2:12).

Our responsibility as ambassadors of Christ is not to justify ourselves to the world, but to be salt and light to the world, knowing that one day the Christ, whom we serve and represent, will come and take his rightful place. Knowing also that on that same day, "At the name of Jesus every knee (will) bow, in heaven and on earth and under the earth, and every tongue confess that Jesus Christ is Lord, to the glory of God the Father" (Phil. 2:10, 11).

The fact is the world will either hate us or love us. However, if it hates us, let it not be because we are hypocrites, but let it be because we unashamedly and unapologetically stand for the truth. If it loves us, let it not be because we go out of our way to do all can do to make it easy for the world to love us, but let it be because we so represent Christ as his ambassadors that the world is attracted, not only to us, but to Christ, by what it sees.

Sadly there are those who claim to represent Christ, but they bring shame to the name of Jesus and they cause men to curse God because of their immoral and questionable lifestyle. But when you live as a true ambassador of Christ, the Apostle Peter confirms that: "(Men will) see your good deeds and will glorify God" (1 Peter 2:12).

So as Jesus declared that **you** are the salt of the earth and that **you** are the light of the world, we need to understand that he is speaking about us and that as Christians, as Christ followers, we are responsible to represent him as ambassadors of influence. God knows the world needs such an influence, and needs us to be salt and light. Governments are filled with spin and sleaze; people are filled with fear and despair; the news is filled with gloom and war; and into the midst of all of this we are sent as ambassadors of Christ to be salt and light; to be ambassadors of influence who will not only be different, but who will truly make a difference.

We live in a world where, despite technological achievement and positive advances, society's moral status has changed little. As someone once said; "At the heart of the human problem, is the problem of the human heart". We might be sending satellites deeper into the cosmos; we might be putting technology at the finger tips of every child who has the blessing of being able to attend school and college; we might be able to run faster and jump higher than those who have gone before us; but the fact remains, man's basic nature has not changed.

World governments are still corrupt to the core as many politicians serve themselves at the expense of those who elected them, and even those who did not. Hitler might well be dead and gone, but the demons that controlled him are still lurking around our world. They are in Africa, including Zimbabwe, Sudan, and Kenya, to name but a few.

Equally, these same demonic forces are in Asia, including India, Pakistan, China, North Korea, and Tibet, to name but a few. They are also in the Middle East, including Iran, Saudi Arabia, Iraq, Afghanistan, and even Israel. They are in Eastern, Central and Western Europe, including Moscow, London, Belfast, and Dublin; they are in America, including Washington DC, New York and San Francisco etc. In some places the corruption and the destructive influences of demonic forces are more evident than in others.

Yet it is into this we are sent to be ambassadors of influence. We are called to be salt in a world that is often corrupt from the mean streets of the inner city to the top seats of bureaucracy. We are called to be light in a world that is just as dark in America as it is in Africa.

Ambassadors of Influence are salt

When salt is added to cooking it brings out the flavour of the food, but even then the recipient might decide to add more salt. For example, when you attend a wedding reception you are normally served soup as a starter to the meal. It is noticeable that right across the reception people are adding salt to their soup, even though salt would have been added to it as it was being cooked.

Ambassadors of influence are to be the salt of the earth and thereby help bring out the best in people and in society. I remember when I first became a Christian I would return home after being at church. My dad at times would have had friends at home playing cards, drinking beer, and using the normal curse words. For the first few weeks of being a new Christian nothing changed at home whenever I showed up. However, after a few weeks, when they saw I was really serious about being a

Christian, things began to change. They continued to play cards and drink beer, but there came the point that whenever someone swore, my dad would say to them, "Hey, cut that out, Jackie's here".

I did not understand it then, neither did they, but I was being an Ambassador of Influence and helping to bring out the best in them. I can only imagine that you have also experienced something similar in your life as a Christian, that when you enter into someone's company, either at work, or at school, or elsewhere within the community, people respect your presence, which is often evidenced by the fact that the direction and the content of the conversation changes.

Salt has many uses and qualities. It not only brings out the best in food in terms of flavour, but also helps to create thirst and makes people want to drink. Jesus made people thirsty by his lifestyle and by his ministry. People were drawn to him, because they knew he had something they lacked. When Jesus met with the woman at the well outside the city of Sychar, he knew there was a definite lack in her life and he said to her, "Whoever drinks the water I give him will never thirst. Indeed, the water I give him will become in him a spring of water welling up to eternal life" (John 4:14). As ambassadors of influence our very lifestyle should be such that it causes people to say, "I want what you have".

Ambassadors of Influence add value to the community

Everyone has an agenda. Churches, community groups, political groups etc, all have their own agendas. Sometimes these agendas are so self-centred that it's not about what can I do for the community, but what can the community do for me. Jesus added value to people; he added value to communities, and as his ambassadors we should be adding value to those around us.

We should be adding value to our communities, and be doing so at every level of community life, e.g. education, health, social care, community development, reconciliation, employment, fair trade businesses, and real politics etc.

This is also borne out by the fact that salt is a precious commodity with its own intrinsic value. Not every country produces salt, but every country needs salt. Every day, each of the earth's six billion plus inhabitants use salt. The annual production of salt is presently over 240 million tons. The leading salt producing nation is China with a production of almost 50 million tons per annum, followed by the USA with a production of 46 million tons; Germany 19; India 16; Canada 15; with other countries holding up the rear with less, but still adding value to their economy.

The fact is humans need salt to survive. Without it we would die. It is essential for good health. The following are just some examples of this: Salt (sodium chloride) is used in some instances to cleanse wounds; it helps to combat hypothermia; expectant mothers are often advised to ensure they take sufficient salt; it has been used successfully to combat Chronic Fatigue Syndrome; it triggers the production of saliva and of gastric juices essential for food digestion; the chemical requirements of the human body demand that the salt concentration in the blood be kept constant; it is effective in stabilizing irregular heartbeats; it is vital to the extraction of excess acidity in brain cells and helps improve the communication and information process all the time that the brain cells work; it is vital for the clearance of the lungs from mucus and phlegm; for clearing up catarrh and congestion of the sinuses; it is essential to making the structure of bones firm; it is vital for preventing varicose veins and spider veins on the legs and thighs; it is vital for sleep regulation as a natural hypnotic; and hey, get this guys, it is vital for maintaining the sex drive.

All of this makes salt essential and valuable. This is why those countries that do not produce salt must purchase it from those that do. Every day there are 1,000s of tons of salt traversing the oceans around us and the skies above us. Getting salt to people does not only add monetary value to those who produce it and sell it, but the salt also adds value and quality of life to those who receive it. As ambassadors of Christ we are the salt of the earth, bringing value to our communities and to our world by being ambassadors of influence promoting new life and encouraging good health.

Ambassadors of Influence sometimes sting

There are times when salt can cause pain when added to a wound, or can cause nausea when too much is taken at any given moment. As ambassadors of Christ our influence can sometimes irritate and sting people, because of their lifestyle, and can sometimes cause people to nauseate, because they cannot stomach our influence. This is what happened with John the Baptist who rubbed Herod up the wrong way. Herod could not stand the truth that came from the mouth of such a man of influence that Herod turned on John and finally had him put to death. The same could be said of Jesus and how his very presence nauseated the Pharisees; and of how Paul was an irritant to the Emperor Nero, the original fiddler on the roof.

We live in a world where political correctness has long since stepped over the thin line from sanity to insanity. We live in a world where political correctness has itself joined the ranks of the insane; a statement which in itself is probably politically incorrect, and if it's not, it might be now! However, ambassadors of Christ do not go out of their way to be offensive, but when they take their place within the community and within the world as ambassadors of Christian influence, like salt that stings and nauseates, their very presence and the stand they take for Biblical truth will likewise irritate and cause nausea to those who live in contradiction to the Word of God. Offence therefore will be unavoidable.

Ambassadors of Influence are light

The Bible tells us that Jesus is the light of the world, yet in sending us out as his ambassadors he tells us that not only are we the salt of the earth, but that we are the light of the world. Do you know that as ambassadors of Christ we are something that John the Baptist was not? That something is light; for it is said of John the Baptist, "He himself was not the light; he came only as a witness to the light" (John 1:8), but Jesus said of us, "You are the light of the world" (Matt. 5:14).

Light is so awesome and so powerful that when it shines, it not only shines in the darkness, but it actually dispels the darkness. You can have a whole lot of darkness and just a little bit of light, but the little bit of light will cut through the thickest of darkness and will be seen by the naked eye. Just a little bit of light is enough to shine through the darkest darkness.

On an aeroplane, when a member of the cabin crew demonstrates the use of the life vest, he or she shows a little torch connected to the side of the vest while it is being explained that if we need to evacuate in water the little torch will automatically light up so we (or our dead bodies) can be detected from the air. Just a little bit of light is enough to potentially save your life, or, if you're not so fortunate, to reveal the location of your floating body.

We live in a world described in the Bible as a place of darkness. This means we have ample opportunity as ambassadors of influence to be light wherever we go, and is why Jesus told us to go into all the world. The earth might look like a big blue marble to those living on Neptune, but it is full of darkness, and it is into this darkness we are sent to be light, with the clear instruction from Jesus telling us not to hide our light, but to let it shine before men that they might see our good deeds and glorify God, because of what they see in us.

This surely is the desired result, that men would glorify God. It is not about the promotion of self; it is not about demonstrating how good we think we are, and neither is it about upsetting people, although that might well be the outcome at times, but the desired result is that men would glorify God.

Pastor Jack Hayford is a man I greatly respect, having been to his church during my first visit to the USA to a leader's conference in 1985, having listened to him preach many times and having met with him personally on one occasion. Among many valuable things that Jack Hayford said was, "The call of the church has never been to be a political analyst. We are called to be cultural catalysts who will act as salt and light in society; but there are dangers; salt if you use too much becomes embittering, and light is annoying if it glares in your face".

In other words, we are not called to be a public nuisance. We are not called to turn people off God or against God or even against us, but our calling, as ambassadors of influence, is to be salt that adds value and to be light that gives direction.

If we behave as true ambassadors of Christ; as true ambassadors of influence, we will not drive people away. We will not repel them, but we will attract and draw them to Christ, and in so doing they will glorify God. As light we will not only show them where they are, but we will also show them where they need to be and show them how to get there.

However, we desperately need to understand where this begins, for it begins within the church. The fact of the matter is, if we cannot be a God-influence to fellow Christians, particularly those within our local fellowship, then how on

God's earth are we going to be a God-influence in our communities and our cities? If we cannot help those in the household of faith when we see a need, then how in a month of Sundays can we genuinely do what is required to meet the needs of the world? If we cannot be salt and light to each other as Christians, then how can we possibly even flicker like fire flies in a darkened world?

For example, even as you read this, think of someone in your home church who is ill right now. Pause for a moment and simply think about that person; just one person. Now let me ask, what have you done to show you really care about that person? Now think of someone you know who is in prison, and without getting all self righteous and going off on a condemnation trip saying "They shouldn't have done what they did in the first place" etc, let me just invite you to pause for a moment and ask, when did you last show that person you really cared about them? When did you last visit them? When did you even send them a card? Now think of someone who has a serious financial need, and let me again ask, when did you show you really cared? When did you do something to help? What have you done to help?

I will finish this chapter with some of the most challenging verses in the entire Bible. These verses are taken from Matthew 25 where Jesus said, *"When the Son of Man comes in his glory, and all the angels with him, he will sit on his throne in heavenly glory. All the nations will be gathered before him and he will separate the people one from another as a shepherd separates the sheep from the goats. He will put the sheep on his right and the goats on his left. Then the King will say to those on his right, 'Come, you who are blessed by my Father; take your inheritance, the kingdom prepared for you since the creation of the world. For I was hungry and you gave me something to eat, I was thirsty and you gave me something to drink, I was a stranger and you invited me in, I needed clothes and you clothed*

me, I was sick and you looked after me, I was in prison and you
came to visit me. Then the righteous will answer him, 'Lord,
when did we see you hungry and feed you, or thirsty and give
you something to drink? When did we see you a stranger and
invite you in or needing clothes and clothe you? When did we
see you sick or in prison and go to visit you?' The King will
reply, 'I tell you the truth, whatever you did for one of the least
of these brothers of mine, you did for me.' Then he will say to
those on his left, 'Depart from me, you who are cursed, into the
eternal fire prepared for the devil and his angels. For I was
hungry and you gave me nothing to eat, I was thirsty and you
gave me nothing to drink, I was a stranger and you did not invite
me in, I needed clothes and you did not clothe me, I was sick and
in prison and you did not look after me.' They also will answer,
'Lord, when did we see you hungry or thirsty or a stranger or
needing clothes or sick or in prison, and did not help you?' He
will reply, 'I tell you the truth, whatever you did not do for one
of the least of these, you did not do for me.' Then they will go
away to eternal punishment, but the righteous to eternal life"*
(Matt. 25:31-46).

The fact is ambassadors of Christ will do as Christ would do;
they will be ambassadors of reconciliation and ambassadors of
influence by being salt and light.

4

Ambassadors of Character

The fruit of the Spirit is love, joy, peace, patience, kindness, goodness, faithfulness, gentleness and self-control. Against such things there is no law. Those who belong to Christ Jesus have crucified the sinful nature with its passions and desires. Since we live by the Spirit, let us keep in step with the Spirit. Let us not become conceited, provoking and envying each other (Gal 5:22-26).

Who is responsible within the Kingdom of God for showing what it means to be a Christian? Who is responsible to reveal and demonstrate how Christians should live before God and before men? Who is responsible for showing how Christians should speak and how they should behave? Is it the Baptists? Is it the Episcopalians? Is it the Methodists? Is it the Pentecostals? (Sorry I do not have sufficient space to add more name tags, so

I'll stop with the Pentecostals, because that's where God stopped – (Come on – it's just a joke!).

Stand Up and Step Up

The fact of the matter is, as a Christian, whatever your church or denomination, it is your responsibility. Every other Christian has their part to play, and are equally responsible as his ambassadors to reveal Christ and to reflect his character. No Christian should be looking to others to fulfil this responsibility to their own exclusion, and no church should be looking to other churches to stand up and be counted as ambassadors of Christian character without looking to themselves first.

It is not up to the Christian who lives across the street. It is not up to the Christian with an elevated title like pastor or elder, and if that's not elevated enough then try 'bishop'. It is not up to the bishop; it is not up to the Christian husband or the Christian wife. But it is up you and your church. So 'don't just sit there', but stand up, step up and be identified as ambassadors of Christ and as ambassadors of Christian Character who not only tell it as it is, but who live the life as it ought to be lived.

When Jesus had indicated to Peter the kind of death he (Peter) would experience, Peter looked over at young John and said, "What about him?" Jesus immediately responded by saying, "If I want him to remain alive until I return, what is that to you? You must follow me" (John 21:21, 22). In other words, 'Mind your own business Peter'. It is interesting to note that of the four writers of the Gospels, John was the only one who recorded this discussion. It is also interesting to note that of all the disciples, John lived into his 90s and witnessed in vision the return of Christ, which he recorded in the book of Revelation.

It is easier to look at others than it is to look at self. It is easier to highlight the shortcomings and faults of others than it is to highlight the faults of self. It is easier to have a greater expectation of others than of self. It is easier to preach ten sermons, or to sing ten songs, than it is to live one. For this reason it is easier to come across as falsely pious, than it is to truly represent Christ as his ambassador, thus leaving ourselves open to the accusation of hypocrisy and of giving people enough reason to criticise.

Failure to be true ambassadors of Christian character gives rise to negative comments against the church, as in the case of Mahatma Ghandi who said, "I like your Christ, but I do not like your Christians, because your Christians are so unlike your Christ".

Belief and Behaviour

Someone might say, "Well Jack, as long as I believe all the right things, then surely that's all that matters; as long as I believe what the Bible says about love, joy and peace; as long as I believe what the Bible says about attitudes and forgiveness; as long as I believe all the right stuff, then that's all that matters."

Well this might rock your world just a little, but we all need to understand that belief and behaviour is not the same thing. You can believe exercise is good for your health, but unless you get up from the potato couch, your belief in health will not suffice to make you healthy! You can believe that smoking cigarettes and inhaling nicotine is bad for your health, yet continue to smoke 20 to 40 a day (perhaps more).

You can believe that getting out to church to fellowship with other Christians is good for your spiritual growth, yet fail to be at church as often as you know you need to be. You can believe that reading the Bible and spending time in the presence of God is essential for your development as a Christian, yet seldom pick up your Bible and seldom enter the quiet place to spend some quality time with God.

There is something about human nature and the human psyche that causes us to believe one thing and yet do another, and the fact is, this same mindset is in us as Christians. We believe one thing, yet do another, which is oftentimes the opposite of what we say we believe; thus my reason for saying that belief and behaviour are not the same.

However, as ambassadors of Christ we are called to be ambassadors of Christian character and as such to live a lifestyle that is compatible with what we say we believe, so that how we behave is not a contradiction to what we say; that we are not saying one thing and doing another; doing the opposite.

For the same reason I would state that faith and works are not the same. That's why James said, "In the same way, faith by itself, if it is not accompanied by action, is dead" (James 2:17). It is also why Jesus said we will know those who are true believers, not by what they say, but by what they do. If I showed you a picture of a banana and asked if you could tell me what kind of tree it came from, you would not say an apple tree or a pear tree. You would tell me, without hesitation, it came from a banana tree, although some might want to argue for a plant rather than a tree!

If I did my utmost to convince you that the banana grew on an apple tree you would not be fooled, because the sight of the banana would be enough to convince you that it grew on a banana tree or a banana plant. I could try to convince you of one thing, but the evidence would be saying something else and would be speaking much louder than the unconvincing words. You see it is not what you say you believe that displays Christian character; it is how you behave.

The Importance of being Earnest!

So belief is not the same as behaviour, and faith is not the same as works. However, although faith and works are not the same,

Christian faith and Christian works are interdependent on each other, because faith is what you have; whereas works are what you do because of what you have. In other words, if you have Christian faith you will demonstrate this by Christian works. You will not seek to do Christian works in order to obtain faith, but you will do Christian works because you have faith. You might need to read this paragraph again; I did!

So faith is what you have, whereas works are what you do, but let me add one word of caution. Do not be fooled into believing that what you do pleases God, because God is not pleased just by works, and neither is he pleased just because you do the right thing. You see it is possible to do the right thing, but to do so with the wrong motive.

It is possible to preach great sermons on the platform, yet not live correctly off the platform. It is possible to be doing the right things in church, yet be a lousy husband and a rotten father at home (this applies to wives and children also). It is possible to be raising your hands in worship on Sunday, but using your hands at work on Monday for things that contradict worship. Doing the right things on Sunday does not cut ice with God if you are purposely doing wrong things on Monday. Doing the right things in church are meaningless if they are done with a wrong motive, and if they are not matched by what you do the rest of the week.

That is why Christian character is so important, because Christian character is not just about what we do or what we are in church, but is about who we are and what we have become in Christ. It is about the kind of person we are, rather than the kind of preacher we are, or the kind of elder we are, or deacon, or worship leader, or singer, or song writer etc. That is why to please God you do not need to become a pastor or a telly evangelist, but you will please God by becoming an ambassador of Christian character, not only in church, but in the home, at school, work, rest and play.

So the focus of those who are ambassadors of Christ should not be on what they do or on how they do what they do, but on why they do what they do and on who they are in Christ and how they represent Christ in the world. This not to say that what we do is not important. Of course it is, and how we do what we do is also important. The fact is we should seek to do all things right and all things well, but with a pure motive to serve and to represent Jesus. We should pursue excellence and effectiveness, but not at the expense of Christian character.

The fact is God is more concerned in 'who' you are and in what you have become, or are becoming, than in what you do in terms of works and skills. The moment a parent becomes more concerned about what their child does, rather than who the child is, is the moment when that parent loses sight of the need for real character. And you need to know that God is more interested in the character of the preacher than in the sermons he preaches. He is more interested in the character of the worship leader than in his ability to lead worship. God is more interested in the character of the sound technician than in his ability to twiddle a few knobs; God is more interested in the character of a deacon than in his ability to deacon; God is more interested in the character of an elder than in his ability to do elder things (not Mafia things!), and God is more interested in the character of the Christian than in his or her ability to do Christian things.

When Paul wrote his letter to the Galatians, he did so because they were confused by the influence of religious Jews who were saying it was not enough to simply believe, but that they needed to add works to their faith, in keeping with the Law of Moses, in order to secure God's forgiveness. One of these laws was circumcision, but the fact that the Galatians were Gentiles did not seem to figure in the minds of these religious Jews who sought only to undermine the work already done by Paul in seeking to impose their religious observances on those who were new converts to the Christian faith.

So Paul writes in an attempt to clear up the mess. At one point he accused the religious Jews of throwing the Galatians into confusion and of perverting the Gospel of Christ. He then said to his readers, "You foolish Galatians! Who has bewitched you?" (Gal. 3:1). He went on to say, "Are you so foolish? After beginning with the Spirit, are you now trying to attain your goal by human effort?" (Gal. 3:3).

You see it is not so much about what you do, but is more about who you are and what you have become in Christ. It is more about character than titles, gifts and abilities, and dare I say it is more about character than it is about VOTES! I personally am not that interested in people because they hold positions as a result of votes acquired, but I am more interested in Christian character. That is why Jesus said, "By this all men will know that you are my disciples, if you love one another" (John 13:35). Not by the fact that we go to church, or that we hold a position in church, but because of our love for (our attitude towards) one another.

Christian love is the first aspect of the Fruit of the Spirit, which is detailed by Paul in Gal. 5, and which will become a major part of this book, spanning chapters 5 to 13. The fact is the Fruit of the Spirit is the outworking of Christian character, because both are interdependent. It's like love and marriage and a horse and carriage, you cannot have one without the other! Well perhaps you can, but they go well together! So ambassadors of Christ, as a consequence of their commitment to Christ, should exhibit the Fruit of the Spirit, and they will do so by being ambassadors of Christian character.

Flesh and Spirit

However, no one said it would be easy. This is why Paul explained to the Galatians that there are two kinds of people, and in fact two kinds of Christians. There are those who live according to the flesh, and there are those who live according to the spirit. The latter have made a conscious choice to become true ambassadors of Christ, and therefore become ambassadors of Christian character in whose lives the Fruit of the Spirit becomes evident. Paul further explained that in all of us a battle is raging between the flesh and the spirit. Yet, while not perfect, ambassadors of Christ will have the strength of character to push through to victory.

Please note there are not nine separate fruits of the Spirit, but there is one fruit that is manifest in the life of the believer in nine different ways. This means that you cannot pick one and leave the rest. You cannot take those aspects of the fruit of the Spirit that you might be more comfortable with and those you prefer more than the others. It is not like going into a fruit shop or a store where you can pick a banana and leave the apples, or you can pick an orange and leave the grapes.

Once you become rooted in Christ you cannot pick love and leave kindness; you cannot pick joy and leave patience etc, but as a true ambassador of Christian character a measure of every aspect of the fruit will become evident in your life. I say measure, because some aspects may be more evident than others, but all will be evident in and through your life as you walk before God and before men.

I suppose another difference between the fruit you purchase in the local fruit shop and the fruit of the Spirit is that in the store you get to pick the fruit you want to purchase, whereas you do not get to pick the fruit of the Spirit at all, you simply grow it. You cultivate it and you grow it within your life. However, in order for this fruit to grow there needs to be a root; and the root of the fruit of the Spirit is Christ himself.

So we need to understand that it is not possible to produce the fruit of the Spirit if we are not firmly rooted to Christ, because every aspect of the fruit of the Spirit is in Christ. If you want the goodness that is in the ground you need to be rooted to what is in the ground. If you want the goodness that is in Christ, you need to be firmly rooted to Christ.

Cultivating the Fruit

Being rooted in Christ is one thing, but cultivating, watering and developing the fruit of the Spirit is another thing. So how do we do this? We do so by giving the Holy Spirit the opportunity to work in our lives by spending quality time with Christ in the secret place to pray to God, to worship God, and to study the Word of God. Not forgetting the need to spend quality time with other believers who are likewise grounded and rooted in Christ by becoming actively involved in the life of the local church; by recognising who you are in Christ and by doing all you can do to become the same person at home, at work, at school, and in the wider community as you are at church.

If you want to be a true ambassador of Christ, you need to be an ambassador of reconciliation; an ambassador of influence and an ambassador of Christian character so that as people simply see how you live they will know by the evidence, by what is produced in your life, the kind of tree you are connected to. Jesus said, "By this all men will know that you are my disciples, if you love one another" (John 13.35).

The world will identify you as a disciple of Christ, not by your singing; not by your preaching; not by your dress code; not by the size of the Bible you carry to church; not by the position you hold in church; nor by the formal title you had conferred upon you as a result of your 'hard earned' votes, but by the fruit of the Spirit.

For this reason I encourage you to get grounded in Christ. 'Don't just sit there'. Put your roots down deep and as a consequence you will develop such strength of Christian character it will enable you to be a true ambassador of Christ.

The following reading serves as a constant warning to all of us:

"Watch out for false prophets. They come to you in sheep's clothing, but inwardly they are ferocious wolves. By their fruit you will recognize them. Do people pick grapes from thorn bushes, or figs from thistles? Likewise every good tree bears good fruit, but a bad tree bears bad fruit. A good tree cannot bear bad fruit, and a bad tree cannot bear good fruit. Every tree that does not bear good fruit is cut down and thrown into the fire. Thus, by their fruit you will recognize them. Not everyone who says to me, 'Lord, Lord,' will enter the kingdom of heaven, but only he who does the will of my Father who is in heaven. Many will say to me on that day, 'Lord, Lord, did we not prophesy in your name, and in your name drive out demons and perform many miracles?' Then I will tell them plainly, 'I never knew you. Away from me, you evildoers!' Therefore, everyone who hears these words of mine and puts them into practice is like a wise man who built his house on the rock" (Matt.7:15-24).

5

Ambassadors of Christian Love

If I speak in the tongues of men and of angels, but have not love, I am only a resounding gong or a clanging cymbal. If I have the gift of prophecy and can fathom all mysteries and all knowledge, and if I have a faith that can move mountains, but have not love, I am nothing. If I give all I possess to the poor and surrender my body to the flames, but have not love, I gain nothing. Love is patient, love is kind. It does not envy, it does not boast, it is not proud. It is not rude, it is not self-seeking, it is not easily angered, it keeps no record of wrongs. Love does not delight in evil but rejoices with the truth. It always protects, always trusts, always hopes, always perseveres. Love never fails. (1 Cor.13:1-8).

There was a band back in the 1980's called Foreigner who had a hit song entitled 'I wanna know what love is'. Now I fully understand that this is just a song. But I think it is symptomatic of the fact that many people do not know what love really is. Even the young Oliver Twist, as he sat looking out the window, thinking about the mother he never knew and wondering if she was out there somewhere, sang a song that asked the question, 'Where is love?' The fact is the world is, and even Christians are, often confused about love.

We talk about 'making love' and about 'Puppy Love' and about 'Mature Love'. We even talk about 'Loving cats'; although why anyone would love cats is beyond me! We talk about loving dogs and cars and loving country and flag and so on. Yet in reality, people are often confused about what love really is. Little children who are abused by those they trust and are being told the abuse is love become confused about the real meaning of love.

Even the highly respected John Maxwell, in my opinion, is somewhat confused about love. I say this with the utmost admiration for one of the greatest teachers in the modern church. However, he did say, "You cannot lead people without loving them". As I considered this comment I thought about Adolf Hitler who led a lot of people, yet loved very few.

What we need to understand is that when we talk about ambassadors of love, we are in reality talking about Christian love. We are not talking about human love whether it is Eros, from which we get the word erotic as it describes passionate sexual love nor 'philos' that describes non-sexual brotherly love or love between friends; neither are we referring to 'storge' that describes the unadulterated love of parents for their children.

The Highest Form of Love

We are talking about 'agape', which is the highest form of love possible, because it is a love that is not self-seeking, but seeks rather the highest good for others, whether friend or foe. Agape, this Christian love, is not a love that depends on 'lovey dovey' feelings. It does not depend on goose bumps or a tingly sensation down one's back, but is about making a choice to seek someone's highest good regardless of who they are or what they have done despite the absence of any tingly sensation, or any other sensation for that matter.

You see when Jesus told us to love one another and even to love our enemies, he was not telling us to go all starry eyed and weak at the knees when we look at each other. He was telling us to make a choice that will enable us to seek the highest good for each other. This is a love that is incomparable with any other form of human love. For this reason we need to be careful about the kind of songs we sing regarding our relationship with Christ, because we are not talking about human love that wants to embrace and kiss, but a love that wants to do the best for Christ and for others.

Now because 'agape' is Christian love and because it is the highest form of love, 'agape' is therefore God's love. This is how God loves. His love for us is his desire for our highest good. He does not love us because we make him go weak at the knees, or because he thinks we are cute, but God loves us insofar as he desires the best for us; he desires our highest good, and he does so whether he thinks we are cute or not.

You see, human love is based on basic human feelings, but the first thing we need to understand about 'agape,' Christian love, is that it is not dependent on human feelings, but upon choice. It is not about going all giddy; it is not about going weak at the knees; it is not about going off your food; it is not about wrapping yourself around someone and seeking self pleasure in doing so; but it is about making the choice to unselfishly seek the highest good for others and is about treating others equally and as equals.

This is why Jesus can command us to love one another and even to love our enemies, because 'agape' is about choice, not about feelings. Jesus could not command us to have 'lovey dovey' feelings for each other, never mind for our enemies. But he can and does command us to seek the highest good for others. That's agape; that's Christian love.

Christian love does not treat people differently. It does not see the colour of a person's skin; it does not see the sometimes divisive colours of flags; it does not see friend or foe; it does not see saint or sinner; it does not see leper or clean skin; it does not see clean or dirty; it does not see rich or poor; and does not see gay or straight. This is the kind of love that loves the unlovable and the unlovely, not because of how it feels, but because of choice.

This is why Paul instructs us to "put on love." (Col.3:13) But how do we do this? How do we put on love? We do so by choice, by our actions and by our behaviour towards one another. That is why John said, "Let us not love with words or tongue but with actions and in truth" (1 John 3:18). How can we truly love someone whom we do not really know? Agape! How can we truly love a man in the street who has not showered for months? Agape! How can we love someone who has sought to harm us? Agape! We do so by making the choice to seek the highest good for others and to demonstrate this by our actions.

Agape is Christian Love in Action

How do we love one another as Christians? Do we turn to one another in church when instructed to do so by the pastor or by the worship leader and with our best Sunday voice tell the person next to us that we love them? No! We do so by our actions. When we say or when we sing 'they will know we are Christians by our love', this is nothing to do with hugging and embracing each other, but is everything to do with how we treat each other.

Now I have no problem with people saying they love each other. Neither do I have a problem with people embracing one another as an act of Christian affection. But the point I am making is that 'agape' means much more than a few words and a weekly embrace.

As ambassadors of Christ we should be ambassadors of Christian love and the evidence of this is not simply in what we say or sing, but is in how we respond to each other in loving actions. The Bee Gees sang "It's only words, and words are all I have to take your heart away", yet even they must have known that we need more than words to claim someone's heart.

One man said to his wife, "You know that I love you so much I would die for you". She quickly replied, "You always say that, but you never do it!" However, this could never be said of God who "So loved the world that he gave his only son" (John 3:16).

The fact is 'agape' is an active love that always seeks the highest good for its object. As we have witnessed God's love in action towards us, we need to understand that God expects us to reciprocate this love by acting on his behalf as ambassadors of his love, so that we don't just sit there content to sing love songs to him and about him. Instead we must take hold of God-given opportunities to exhibit his love for the good of others.

When Jesus rose from the dead he drew close to Peter who had denied him three times and, in response to these three denials, three times Jesus asked Peter the question, "Do you love me more than these?" In the first two questions Jesus used the word 'agape' but Peter responded with the word 'philos', which is brotherly love or the love of a friend. Jesus then asked the third question, but this time he used the word that Peter used, philos. It seems that this was a reminder of Peter's denials, which cut Peter to the heart and brought the response, "Lord you know all things", and he once again, for a third time, expressed his love for Christ. However, Jesus was endeavouring to get Peter from 'philos' to 'agape', which is the level of love he wants his ambassadors to attain.

Each time that Peter declared his love for Jesus; he was told to do something, i.e. "Feed my lambs" and "Feed my sheep". Why? Because "Yes I love you" was not enough. So that, ambassadors of Christ are ambassadors of Christian love who represent Christ, not just by what they say, but also by what they do and by the manner of those actions.

In 1 Cor.13 Paul writes some amazing things about Christian love and the word he uses for love is 'agape'. He said, "Love (agape) is patient, love is kind. It does not envy, it does not boast, it is not proud. It is not rude, it is not self-seeking, it is not easily angered, it keeps no record of wrongs. Love does not delight in evil but rejoices with the truth. It always protects, always trusts, always hopes, always perseveres. Love never fails." (1 Cor.13:1-8).

The Gospel is not summed up in sermons or songs, but it is summed up in one verse where Jesus said, "Do to others what you would have them do to you, for this sums up the law and the prophets" (Matt.7:12). The phrase, the law and the prophets, was understood by the Jewish people to mean the Old Testament scriptures or the Word of God. It is often said by preachers that John 3:16 is the Gospel in a nutshell, but Jesus said that the entire teaching of God's Word is wrapped up in doing for others what you would have them do for you.

It is wrapped up in how we treat each other; how we speak to each other and how we speak about each other. When we think we have reason to be negative about someone we need to remember that Paul makes an appeal for love's sake (see Phm. 1:9) and prays that love may abound (see Phil. 1:9). There are some people that you simply have to make allowances for, and because ambassadors of Christ are ambassadors of Christian love they will therefore make the required allowances.

The Essence of Christian Love

I am often challenged by the WWJD (What Would Jesus Do) symbol. With this in mind I want you to imagine that Jesus is in your company when someone, who does not fit into your connect group, walks into the room. Now, imagine what Jesus would do? Could you imagine him whispering, "Hey, look at him" or, "Look at her"? Could you imagine him saying, "Who does he think he is?" or, "Who does she think she is"? Could you imagine him beginning to gossip and say things like, "Did you hear about so and so"? No, friends. Jesus is higher than that, and so too are his ambassadors.

You see the essence of Christian love is not about singing love songs to Jesus, but is about doing what Jesus would do and that is to think less of self and more of others even when you run the risk of being mocked and branded as the weakest link by others. The essence of Christian love is doing for others what you would have them do for you. The essence of Christian love is doing 'What Jesus Would Do'.

An ambassador of Christ takes seriously the words of Jesus when he said, "If anyone would come after me, he must deny himself, and take up his cross and follow me" (Matt. 16:24). The essence of Christian love is not about how much money you can sow to see how much you can get back, particularly when you are being manipulated by those who want you to believe that God will not bless you if you do not sow into their ministry. The essence of Christian love is self sacrifice, by denying self and by being willing to sell all you have, for the cause of Christ and for the good of others. So come on, don't just sit there, but become an ambassador of Christian love by doing for others what you would have them do for you, even though they do not deserve it, and with the risk of having it thrown back in your face.

I remember being involved in helping one particular person in more ways than one and in some incredible ways beyond the call of duty for any pastor. He had often disappointed me, but I continued to believe and hope for the best. Others expressed their concerns at my willingness to continue to help, but help I did. Then one day he turned on me with venom. So although this finally led to a parting of the ways, I still had to listen to "I told you so" comments several times from those who were close to me, but they knew my heart and my motives.

However, several months later this same person came to see me. He was in very serious trouble. He admitted to me at the time that he "had a brass neck in coming to me", but there was no one else he could turn to. Three men, well known members of a terrorist organisation, were waiting for him to bring money to them that he had owed and had failed to pay in time to a local businessman. He had the money to hand over, but wanted me to go with him in case something went wrong.

Some of my associates watched in bewilderment as I took him in my car to meet with these men. I drove to a garage (gas station) on the Shankill Road where the men were waiting at the back of the premises. I sat in the car while the person with me got out and met with these men and handed over the money. I watched through my mirror as fingers were being pointed and angry words were being issued from them. When he got back into the car he asked me to drive away quickly. He explained that one man had a gun and had intended shooting him, but did not do so because I was with him. Now this person did not deserve this from me, but Christian love is not about what someone deserves. Christian love is about doing 'What Jesus Would Do', which is exactly what an ambassador of his is expected to do.

6

Ambassadors of Christian Joy

Paul said, "Rejoice in the Lord always and again I say rejoice" (Phil. 4:4)

We all know what it is to have a bad day; even on a Sunday! Perhaps you are reading this book at a time when this has not been a good day for you. Your alarm clock seemed to go off too early or your toaster did not go off early enough. Perhaps someone had used the last piece of toothpaste or you had a flat tyre and were 30 minutes late for work. Maybe you did not get that promotion you were hoping for, but your neighbour did; and so on.

The fact is we all experience days when nothing seems to go right, or it seems that no matter how hard you try to do what is right and to please those around you, whether at work or even in church, there are some people you can just never please. To top it all, when you are driving home from church you come off your motorbike, but thankfully it happens outside a Baptist church where some of your spiritual relatives come to your rescue (this did happen to one of our guys), and when you finally get home the chicken is wearing sunglasses and looks more like a burnt offering than an appetising Sunday dinner.

Or perhaps you're on the buses and you're driving a 'double decker' through Belfast. It's been a good day thus far. The passengers have been on their best behaviour. The sun is shining and the sky is as blue as your standard issue busman's shirt. Everything is going well until you turn into Castle Lane, and you forget you are driving a 'double decker'. You pull in to pick up several passengers waiting in the comfort zone of the bus shelter. All are totally oblivious to the fact that they are about to enter the twilight zone and that soon their plans for the day would be every bit as shattered as the shelter around them, caused by the upper deck of the bus ripping through it (this did happen to one of our guys).

Maybe you have had a row with your wife or with someone else's wife or husband. Maybe your child or the neighbour's dog kept you awake for most of last night, but you have picked up this book and you have turned to this chapter, and you are reading about 'Christian Joy'!" And you are thinking to yourself, "It is not so easy Jack; it has not been a good day you know!"

When circumstances go bad

Well what about when something really bad happens? Imagine being arrested for your faith and being thrown into prison. Imagine being beaten just because you are a Christian. Imagine someone in your family dies suddenly or has been killed for being a Christian. Imagine when the child does not cry at night, or that your wayward offspring does not come home late in the evening. Imagine you get that phone call we all dread and fear might someday happen. Imagine when something really bad happens! I fully understand that some who may be reading this book right now do not need to imagine some of the above, because some of you have been there.

Yet it is into the midst of all of this that Paul said, "Rejoice in the Lord always, and again I say rejoice" (Phil. 4:4). The reality is that in spite of all we go through, one of the things we cannot get away from is the fact that God wants each one of us to be blessed. He wants his people to be a blessed people, and he tells us through the Psalmist David how to be blessed, for David said, "Blessed is the man who does not walk in the counsel of the wicked or stand in the way of sinners or sit in the seat of mockers. But his delight is in the law of the Lord" (Psalm 1:1, 2).

So the source of Christian Joy is found first of all in our ability to take delight in the Word of God and our willingness to walk in obedience to it. We have often been taught that the word blessed means happy, so that when David said, "Blessed is the man" we believe he is saying "Happy is the man". However, I want you to see that to be blessed means much more than being happy, because happy is a superficial feeling that depends on circumstances being right and on everything being good.

For some people, happy is about having lots of other people around them, like friends and family etc. For others, it is money that makes the world go round. For some it is having a nice home that floats their boat. Then there are those who find that having their very own car is a source of happiness, and the bigger the car the happier they are. For many it is having good health; for others it is having freedom; and for others it is buying new clothes (not just having new clothes, but buying them).

But what if all this was gone? What if your friends deserted you? What if you had no family to turn to in your trying and lonely moments of life? What if the stock markets crashed and your money was gone? What if your home was taken from you and you had no home? What if you had no car to park outside your no home? What if your health was failing and you received the worse news possible from your doctor? What if your freedom was taken from you? What if you were no longer in the position to buy new clothes or if you could not remember when you had eaten your last good meal? What if all those things that make you happy, the things that make other people happy, what if they were all gone?

It is my conviction that if all of the above were taken from us, most people would find their happiness would disappear, because for the majority of people happiness depends on having the comforts of life, and the more comforts the merrier they are. For most people, happiness is about having as much stuff as they can take hold of and hold on to without letting go, because for the majority of people, happiness is a surface thing that depends on circumstances and stuff. But David said, "Blessed is the man … whose delight is in the law of the Lord" (Psalm 1:1, 2). Such a person is like a tree planted by streams of water, which yields its fruit in season and whose leaf does not wither, and whatever he does prospers (see Psalm 1:3).

That is why there are some Christians who so love God and who give all they have and all they are to serve God and, they do so though they are physically tortured and run the risk of being killed for their faith in Christ. We would surely struggle to even suggest they are happy. Yet they are probably more blessed than you and I can even begin to imagine because the word blessed means more than superficial happiness that relies on materialistic possessions or on the right physical conditions. Rather it means you have a joy that remains steadfast when everything else is removed.

Rejoice in the Lord always

When Paul wrote his letter to the Philippians he was in prison. He had lost his freedom, yet he could still write "Rejoice in the

Lord always", and, just in case they did not get it the first time he said, "And again I say Rejoice" (Phil.4:4). People on the outside should have been writing to Paul who was inside the prison. They should have been writing to encourage him and to tell him to keep his chin up. Yet he was writing to them telling them to remain joyful.

Paul's health was not the best. In fact he had asked God to remove his problem, a problem he called 'a thorn in the flesh'. But three times God said "No". Still he could write "Rejoice in the Lord always." Most of his friends had deserted him but he could still write "Rejoice in the Lord always." He had no family around him to offer support and to visit him in his time of need, yet he could still write "Rejoice in the Lord always"; he was broke financially more times than we can imagine, often depending on support coming from churches and going out to work when it did not, and yet he could still write "Rejoice in the Lord always".

Now Paul was not saying we should always be 'happy clappy', although there is nothing wrong with being happy clappy. In fact it would do some Christians the world of good to hit themselves a little 'slappy', just as David did when he spoke to himself on no less than three occasions and said, "Why are you cast down, O my soul? And why are you disquieted within me? Hope in God, for I shall yet praise Him for the help of His countenance" (Psalm 42:5; 42:11; 43:5).

However, Paul was not saying we should always be happy clappy, but he is saying we should always be rejoicing, because as Christians, and as ambassadors of Christ we have a joy that does not depend on the stuff of this world, but on our ability and on our willingness to walk in obedience to the Word of God.

The ambassadors of Christ are such ambassadors of Joy they do not need the right atmosphere to help lift them to the point where they feel they can worship God; they do not need the coloured lights (although some churches could do with a few); they do not need the music to be cranked up (although some churches, according to David in Psalm 150, could do with cranking it up a level or two, or even three!). True ambassadors of Christ do not need to know their choice car is sitting outside the front door of the church or that their Lear Jet is sitting close by, ready to whisk them off to their next engagement to the cheers and waves of their onlooking supporters (and you think I'm kidding!).

That is why when Paul was in prison, despite having none of those things that make people happy, he and Silas held a praise service or some kind of Worship Conference; inside the jail! He had no green room, but a dark room (it is amazing what some visiting ministries expect and demand these days!); he had no amplification system with the latest headset microphones. But he did have an echo chamber that carried his voice man-ward and his praise heavenward. He had no lighting system to help set the mood, but he had the light of God's presence that caused the prison darkness to flee. He had no machine to cause haze to waft through the prison, but he had the Holy Spirit who filled the prison and every cell and (more importantly) every life within the prison.

Paul and Silas were happy clappy okay, but they were happy clappy not because everything was good, because they obviously were not, but they were joyful in spite of the fact that nothing seemed to be working out. I tell you, this was more than just happy, but this was joy, and it is the kind of joy that should be in us as ambassadors of Christ.

You see the ambassador of Christ is an ambassador of Christian character, and as such is an ambassador of Christian Love and of Christian Joy. You only need to read through the book of Acts and you will see it is a book filled with stories featuring Christians who, although being persecuted, were full of Joy. They faced the kind of hardships that most Christians in the modern western world know little of, apart from what they read in books and magazines etc. However, some of those early believers in the book of Acts were killed by the sword. Some were brutally stoned to death, others were tortured in a variety of ways and many were cast into prison, never to come out alive. Yet they were full of joy.

David said, "The Lord is my strength, my shield from every danger. I trust in him with all my heart. He helps me, and my heart is filled with joy. I burst out in songs of thanksgiving" (Psalm 28:7). This was their strength. This is what enabled them to give thanks to God in all things, not 'because' of all things, but 'in' all things. Paul was not praising God because of prison, but he was praising God in prison, not because of the fact, but in spite of the fact. Why? Because when Paul had reason to quit, the joy of the Lord was his strength.

There is an old Christian song called 'The Joy of Lord is my strength'. I remember the last verse had simply one word that was repeated over and over again, "_Ha ha ha ha ha ha ha ha ha ha ...". I also recall a time back in my Bible College days, when one particular student drove the rest of us crazy! He drove us up the walls! I will not mention his name for legal reasons, but his first name sounded like the alcoholic drink sherry, and his second name sounded exactly the same as pain, but was spelt differently. Hey, I am just having a little bit of fun, but true!

Anyway, as students we had to do early morning work periods before breakfast. It was hard getting out of bed to be out working around the college by 7.25 am. Some of us thought that God didn't even get up at that time of the morning. However, every morning you could hear this guy at about 7.15 am walking through the college grounds on his merry way to carry out his early morning work duties, and he was doing so while singing at the top of his voice. He was singing the words of the song, "The joy of the Lord is my strength", and then he got to the verse, "Ha ha ha ha ha ha ha ha ha ha ha ha". Man it was so irritating to hear someone happy like that, especially at that ungodly time of the morning.

Now I agree that it brings a smile to your face (the song that is), but that is not what Christian joy is about, because Christian joy is as real when you do not have a smile on your face as the times when you do. The ambassador of Christ is an ambassador of joy who, regardless of the circumstances, is able to rejoice in the Lord always; although, Bible College students are exempt at 7.15 am!

Knowing God is in control

Where did Paul's joy come from? Well it came from his ability to walk in obedience to the Word of God. It was this that enabled him to believe that, no matter about the problems he faced, he still had hope. In writing to the Romans he said, "We joyfully look forward to sharing God's glory" (Rom. 5:2); but then, in the next breath, he says, "We can rejoice, too, when we run into problems and trials" (v.3).

"We can rejoice too"; in other words he was saying that, while we have enough reason to rejoice by looking forward to sharing in God's glory, it is not our only reason to rejoice. Hanna-Barbera used a line at the end of their cartoons, which said, "That's all folks!" but some 2,000 years ago, when there was no concept of cartoons or of some character called Road Runner, Paul was clearly saying, "That's not all folks". He was declaring the fact that we have joy in the hope of the glory of God, but also that it does not end there, for we have even more reason to rejoice than that.

However, while it sounds crazy, Paul is saying we can also rejoice when we run into problems and trials. Why? Well, according to Paul, "They are good for us – they help us learn to endure. And endurance develops strength of character in us, and character strengthens our confident expectation of salvation" (Rom.5:4).

Yet still it does not end there, because Paul goes on to say, "So now we can rejoice in our wonderful new relationship with God – all because of what our Lord Jesus Christ has done for us in making us friends of God" (Rom.5:11). So we rejoice in the hope of sharing in God's glory; we rejoice even in trials, because our trials produce character; and we rejoice in our relationship with God and in knowing Christ.

You see, a person can have all the stuff of this world, yet have no joy because they have no hope and because they do not know Christ. That is why Paul speaks of those who are "In the world, but without hope and without God" (Eph.2:12). However, if it is possible to be in the world without hope and without God, it is also possible to be in the world with hope and with God.

It is possible to have joy in the midst of financial crisis, or when sickness is tearing away at your body, or when it seems like your world is caving in, or when it seems like the forces of darkness are prevailing; to have that same joy of Christ who for the joy that was set before him, endured the cross, knowing that even on the cross God was in control. Likewise, we need to understand that even in the midst of tragedy and pain there is joy in knowing that God is in control.

While preparing this book I received an email from a friend in California. The email read as follows: "We lost one of our dear grandchildren yesterday (3 February 2008) at 11:26 am to pneumonia. He was 4 years old and the light of my life. I don't know what to write. I know that God is in control, but I'm sure having a hard time seeing Him right now. Please pray for our family as we struggle to get through this," Bob and Kay McKee. The painful tragedy in this message is the loss of a precious child, but the key to the message is that even in the midst of the loss and the pain, and though it is difficult to see God at times, you are still able to say, "I know that God is in control."

At the same time as the above email came through, one of our church members, Billy Haddock, received a call that his little grandchild had been rushed into hospital in Scotland. He and his wife immediately got on the ferry to Scotland, but as soon as they got off on the other side he received another call, from their daughter Nicola, informing him the child had died. You can only imagine how distracted he and his wife Agnes were at that time.

They drove to the area where their daughter lived, but then got a little lost. Billy prayed and asked God for help. He then saw a taxi and approached the driver for directions or to get him to drive in front of their car. It turned out the taxi driver was a born again Christian. He led the way to their daughter's home where he embraced Billy as a brother in Christ and assured him of his prayers. When Billy shared this with me on the phone he said, "When I needed help, God sent an angel. This helped me to see that God is in control".

There is just something about knowing that God is in control; about knowing that no matter what happens, no matter the circumstances, or regardless of the individual tragedy, God is still in control. An ambassador of Christ knows that even though it sometimes might not be so easy to see, yet that does not alter the fact that God is in control. This is evident in their character; in their ability and willingness to love as Christ loves and to be ambassadors of Joy when it would be so much easier to quit.

Ambassadors are always observed

Something else we need to understand about ambassadors is that they are being watched. All ambassadors everywhere are under constant observation. Their phones are bugged; they have little hidden cameras in their apartments and homes. They only need to leave their office and they are being filmed and photographed. This might sound a bit 'James Bondish', but it does happen. So keeping this in mind we also need to understand that as ambassadors of Christ we are being watched and listened to, not only by our enemies, but also by our friends, neighbours, work mates and school friends.

We also need to understand that, although the Christian life is not without its problems, people are watching us and witnessing how we live and how we deal with the same problems they face. However, they should see us respond to those problems differently. God declared through the prophet Isaiah, "When you pass through the waters, I will be with you; and when you pass through the rivers, they will not sweep over you. When you walk through the fire, you will not be burned; the flames will not set you ablaze." (Isa.43:2). The fact is God sees the bigger picture, as do the ambassadors of Christ, for they know that God has said, "I will never leave you nor forsake you" (Josh.1:5).

They can say, like Shadrach, Meshach and Abednego, "If we are thrown into the blazing furnace, the God we serve is able to save us from it, and he will rescue us from your hand, O king. But even if he does not, we want you to know, O king, that we will not serve your gods or worship the image of gold you have set up" (Dan.3:17,18).

The bottom line was that as ambassadors of the God they served, they knew that no matter what happened, good or ill, God was still in control. Unforeseen circumstances might cause us great pain and might even take from us those things that are precious to us and even those who are closest to us, but they cannot take from us what God has put within us, including his joy and his peace.

7

Ambassadors of Peace

*Jesus said, "Peace I leave with you; my peace I give
you. I do not give to you as the world gives. Do not let
your hearts be troubled and do not be afraid" (John
14:27).*

The moment we think of peace our minds often imagine some
quiet, idyllic place, hidden in the remotest part of our planet far
away from the disruptive influences of political intrigue and
social turmoil. However, regardless of our imagination, we need
to understand that although Jesus gives us peace, he is not
giving peace 'from' trouble, but rather he is giving peace in the
midst of trouble. As Christians, we are no longer of this world,
but we are in the world, and we are called to minister to the
world, and one of those things we are expected to bring to the
world is peace.

Carriers of peace

As ambassadors of Christ, we are sent as carriers of peace so that we are not to be adding to the world's problems, but contributing to the solutions of its problems. There is a story told by John Maxwell of three world leaders who got together to discuss the subject of world peace. These were Nikita Khrushchev, the President of the USSR; John F Kennedy, the President of the USA; and Golda Meir, the Prime Minister of Israel.

They decided to pray and to ask God what he thought about the possibilities of peace, but each was thinking of peace relating to their particular situations. Nikita Khrushchev, who incidentally had become a Christian while he was President of the USSR, asked God if there would ever be peace between Russia and America, to which God replied, "Not in your lifetime".

John F Kennedy then asked God if there would ever be peace between the blacks and the whites in America, to which God replied, "Not in your lifetime". The third to pray was Golda Meir who asked God if there would ever be peace in the Middle East between the Arabs and the Jews, to which God replied, "Not in my lifetime"!

Now let me make it clear that although Jesus is sending us out as carriers of peace, the purpose is not to bring about world peace during our lifetime or even during the lifetime of the church, but he is sending us out to bring peace into the midst of the world regardless of its circumstances. The fact that we will not establish world peace in our lifetime is clear because Jesus declared that wars and rumours of wars would be prevailing on the earth prior to and up to his return. But we can bring peace into the world by our very presence and by our influence as ambassadors of peace.

When Jesus was born the angels appeared to the shepherds and declared "peace on earth". They did not do this because world peace had been established at that time, because it had not. The Romans were still marching across Europe and across the Middle East. Israel was under Roman control and domination and was governed by a puppet king and a feeble governor. No, world peace did not exist at that time, or at anytime since. The reason the angels declared "Peace on earth" was because Christ, the Prince of Peace, was on earth, having arrived that night in Bethlehem of Judea.

Jesus Christ, the Son of God, was and is the very embodiment of peace and because he was present on earth, peace was also present. As his ambassadors we are sent to represent him, which is one of the reasons the church is described as the body of Christ, because the church is now the embodiment of peace in a world that is being raped and ravaged with conflict and war. It is into this world we are sent to be carriers of his peace.

Peace is not the absence of conflict

The world perceives peace as the absence of conflict, the absence of war, the absence of problems, and the absence of negative issues. The world thinks in terms of – if we can stop the bombings; if we can prevent the shootings; if we can get people to agree with each other; if we can persuade two world leaders to sign the dotted lines in two separate books with a mediator sitting between them; if we can get those who are enemies to put all of their hostilities behind them; and if we can convince people to stop allowing their differences to divide them, then we will have peace.

But even if it was possible to silence the bombs and the bullets etc, this world would still be troubled and men's hearts would continue to fail because of fear; why? The reason is simple, it is because peace is not the absence of war or conflict or problems. The peace the Bible speaks of is the kind of peace that can be known and experienced in the midst of war and conflict. It is a peace that is beyond human reason and understanding so much so that Paul said, "The peace of God, transcends all understanding (Phil. 4:7).

It transcends human peace and world peace. It is a higher form of peace in much the same way that Christian love is a higher form of love than basic human love, because Christian love is not based on feelings, but is based on making a choice to do the highest good for others, even those who are deemed to be our enemies.

It is a higher form of peace in much the same way that Christian joy is a higher form of joy than human joy, because Christian joy is not dependent on circumstances, but is dependent on knowing that no matter what happens, God is in control and is the very reason why Paul says, "Rejoice in the Lord always, and again I say rejoice" (Phil.4:4).

By the same reasoning this is why Jesus declared that the peace he gives is not the peace of this world. The fact is you cannot get this kind of peace in the world or from the world, and nothing that happens in the world can take it from you. This is not the kind of peace that depends on the absence of conflict or war, but is dependent on a living, loving relationship with God through Jesus Christ. As Paul said, "For he himself (Christ) is our peace, who has made the two one and has destroyed the barrier, the dividing wall of hostility" (Eph. 2:14).

In John 16 Jesus told the disciples that he was returning to the father and that when he would do so they would be scattered. He then went on to say, "I have told you these things, so that in me you may have peace. In this world you will have trouble. But take heart! I have overcome the world" (John 16:33). You see this peace is in Christ and is in knowing Christ; it is not in the world, because in the world you will have trouble, but in Christ you will have peace.

How do we get this peace?

We get this peace by first of all knowing Christ. Not by knowing about him, but by knowing him. The fact is you can know about people without ever knowing them personally. We all know about certain famous people; we know about world leaders, but seldom do we ever get to truly know them personally. Yet to know Christ is to know him in reality; to know him in person; to know him in a living relationship; to know him as Lord; to know him as saviour; to know him as friend; and to know him as someone who is always looking out for you.

I remember when I was about 9 years old my dad took me to my very first football match. It was at Windsor Park in Belfast and was between Lindfield (the Blues) and Distillery (the Whites). My dad lifted me over the turnstile so he did not have to pay for me. As I walked with excitement into one of the stands, although I think it was all terraces back then with no seats, I saw the biggest crowd of people I had ever seen in my entire life. There were thousands! It looked to me like the whole population of Belfast was at Windsor Park.

Yet I do not ever remember being afraid. I was excited, but not afraid. I was conscious of the fact that someone bigger than me, my dad, was looking out for me. But in an even greater sense there is peace in knowing Christ personally and in knowing he is watching out for you. Someone said, "Know Christ, Know Peace; No Christ, No Peace".

The second thing we need to do in order to get this peace is to obey the Word of God. It is one thing to know Christ, but it is another thing entirely to walk in obedience to the Word of God. "This is what the Lord says, your Redeemer, the Holy One of Israel: "I am the Lord your God, who teaches you what is best for you, who directs you in the way you should go. If only you had paid attention to my commands, your peace would have been like a river" (Isa.48:17-18).

God is saying, even to us, that if only you had obeyed my word you would have known such an awesome peace. Some think it is enough to sing the song, "I've got peace like a river in my soul", but it is one thing to know the words and to know the song; it is another thing entirely to know the reality of peace in your life because you know Christ and because you are walking in obedience to the Word of God.

If your relationship with Christ is not what it ought to be, then your peace will not be what it could be and what it should be. If your relationship with Christ breaks down, then your peace will also break down. By the same token, when you fail to live and walk in obedience to the Word of God you will not be able to live and walk in peace.

But conversely, when you live and walk in a relationship with Christ and in obedience to the Word of God you will not only live and walk in peace, but you will do so as an ambassador of peace. You will do so regardless of the surrounding circumstances, because you will have acquired a peace within you that does not depend on what is happening around you. There is a sense of wholeness and a sense of wellbeing that is beyond anything this world can offer, which can only be found in knowing Christ and in walking in obedience to the Word of God.

It is this very idea of wholeness and wellbeing that is at the heart of the Hebrew word "Shalom". When you say "Shalom" to someone you are not simply wishing them freedom 'from' conflict, but you are wishing them peace even 'in the midst' of conflict. You are wishing them wholeness and wellbeing in their lives regardless of what is happening elsewhere in the world or in their immediate circumstances.

There is no place on earth where the word shalom is spoken more than in Israel. Everyday families and friends are greeting each other with the word shalom. They are constantly wishing each other peace, yet all around them are those who have purposed to annihilate them. They are living with conflict everyday not knowing if each day would be their last, yet they speak shalom, because in the midst of conflict they believe they can know peace; shalom – wholeness and wellbeing.

You have heard it said, "There is no rest for the wicked", well the original statement is "There is no peace for the wicked". This was actually said by God through the prophet Isaiah (48:22). The reason there is no peace for the wicked is because they do not know Christ and do not live and walk in obedience to the Word of God. According to Paul they are "in the world without hope and without God" (Eph. 2:12), but they are also in the world without peace. So the only way to get this peace is to know Christ personally and to walk in obedience to the Word of God.

God is in control

One of the benefits of this peace is to know that God is always in control. When Jesus was in the boat and a violent storm threatened to destroy the boat and to drown everyone in it, he was asleep at the back of the boat! Why? Because he knew God was in control.

When Paul was facing death for about the ninetieth time he said, "For to me, to live is Christ and to die is gain. If I am to go on living in the body, this will mean fruitful labour for me. Yet what shall I choose? I do not know! I am torn between the two: I desire to depart and be with Christ, which is better by far; but it is more necessary for you that I remain in the body. Convinced of this, I know that I will remain, and I will continue with all of you for your progress and joy in the faith" (Phil 1.21-25).

It seems from these comments that Paul believed he had a choice. Perhaps he did. Perhaps God had said to him that he had suffered enough and it was now time for him to come home. It seemed he could decide between continuing his life on earth or to begin his life in heaven! Either way, to stay or to go, Paul was at peace.

Many have heard the very moving story of Horatio Spafford, the writer of the hymn 'It is well with my soul'. It is worth repeating the story at this point. Horatio Spafford lived in Chicago during the 19th century. He was a successful businessman and property owner. However, a disastrous fire in 1871 wiped out his holdings. Shortly after this he decided to take his family to Europe.

However, due to urgent business, he sent his wife and their four daughters ahead of him, and planned to follow soon afterwards. Tragically, on the night of November 22, 1873, the ship they were sailing in was struck by another ship. It sank within 12 minutes with only 47 surviving of the 273 on board.

Mrs. Spafford, although severely injured, was among the survivors, but sadly her four daughters did not survive. When she reached Cardiff, Wales, she cabled a brief message to her husband, "Saved alone, what shall I do?" Horatio Spafford immediately left for Europe to join his wife. As he crossed the Atlantic Ocean he sailed passed the place where the Ville du Havre had apparently sunk and where his four daughters had lost their lives.

After viewing the spot where his daughters' lives were ended on this earth he returned to his cabin where he sat down and wrote the words, "It is well; the will of God be done." Sometime afterwards he wrote the words of the well known hymn "It Is Well with My Soul". The hymn begins "When peace like a river attendeth my way, when sorrows like sea billows roll, whatever my lot, thou hast taught me to know, it is well, it is well, with my soul.

This man, for all his turmoil, experienced the peace that only Christ could give. This peace did not take away the reality of his loss or the pain of that reality, but it did enable him to declare that when peace like a river attended him, or when sorrows like sea billows came against him, either way, it was well with his soul – a true ambassador of peace.

Peacemakers; not just Peacekeepers

Ambassadors of peace are not those who only experience peace for themselves regardless of the circumstances, and they are not simply keepers of the peace, which of course they ought to be, but they are also peacemakers. The difference between a peacekeeper and a peacemaker is the difference between passivity and activity. A peacekeeper just needs to stay at home and watch television, whereas a peacemaker has heard God say "Don't just sit there" and who responds by getting up and by going and doing what it takes to make peace; to do so when required and to take risks when necessary.

Several times, as a church, we have shown our willingness to take those necessary risks. We were in our third night of a four week prayer walk during a violent and devastating internal paramilitary feud within our community. Midnight was approaching fast, and our Prayer Walk teams were thinking more about home than about anything happening during the remaining moments of the walk.

The night had been tense, but the streets were quiet when suddenly we heard screaming and shouting. The streets of the Lower Shankill had finally come under attack. What looked like a dozen or more cars drove into the neighbourhood and within moments the area was swamped with men from other parts of the community. They fought hand to hand with any who still happened to be in the street at that time.

At the time of the attack I had been sitting in someone's home when I heard the screams of people in the street and immediately made my way to where the fighting had been taking place. In the darkness I could see cars in the middle of the street as if they had been abandoned. They were sitting where they had come to a halt; some with doors lying open, and some with the engine still running.

There were also several military and police vehicles sitting along the street with dozens of heavily armed soldiers and police officers standing alongside. Then I noticed in the darkness that around twenty men were lined along one of the gable walls. These were some of the men who had made the attack. Each man was standing with his hands raised in the air and each had a police officer standing in front of him pointing a gun directly at his head.

As I walked into the middle of this scene, a scene that resembled a remake of a Lethal Weapon movie, I heard someone call out, "Hey Pastor Jack! Pastor Jack!" I immediately froze on the spot and the person continued to shout, "You came to us for help last night and we've done you a favour. Can you do anything to help us?" Puzzled, I looked around, and there standing against the wall was one of two men I had spoken to for almost an hour the previous night.

Now I knew these were members of a terrorist organisation and that they were involved in a feud. I knew that I had often been vocal in my public condemnation of this group for various reasons. I also knew that this same organisation had sentenced me to death on at least one occasion, which I detailed in my first book 'Through Terror and Adversity'. Yet here were some of its men up against a wall and under arrest calling out my name and asking for help! Yet for some reason, and against my better judgement, I felt I needed to do something to help the situation move forward. So I approached the senior police officer in charge, who looked like Darth Vader. As I spoke with him, another police officer, who was standing next to him and listening to our conversation, screamed out the words, "Gun, Gun!"

Immediately on hearing this, 'Darth Vader' ran for cover behind one of his armoured vehicles leaving me standing in the open and in the dark. He was immediately followed by every police officer and every soldier in the street! The twenty men who had been arrested were left standing against the wall. With their hands still in the air they turned and looked at each other with an expression of total bewilderment, but realising they were now on their own they ran to their cars that were still sitting in front of them with doors open and engines running.

I could hardly believe what I was seeing. This was now looking more like a remake of Police Academy (not that I watch such nonsense), but it was really happening. I was still standing on the centre of the road trying to unravel in my mind the things I had seen with my eyes. I had not heard any gunfire. I had not seen any guns other than those being carried by the security forces, yet the police and the soldiers were hiding!

The man who had earlier called out to me for help had also jumped into his car, but before driving away he stopped alongside me and said, "Thanks Jack! You can tell the people in the community that the feud is over; tell them they've nothing to fear now, for we know they've suffered long enough." And with this he drove off. The police officers and the soldiers then came out from behind their vehicles, but the men against the wall were all gone. Soon the police and the soldiers were also gone and within moments the streets were quiet.

Jesus said, "Blessed are the peacemakers, for they will be called sons of God" (Matt. 5:9). He also said, "When you enter a house, first say, 'Peace to this house'" (Luke 10:5). The fact is we are ambassadors of peace who carry his peace in us and with us and when required to do so, we help make peace whenever and however we can. Paul said, "If it is possible, as far as it depends on you, live at peace with everyone" (Rom 12:18). This includes those who are in the church, those who are of the household of faith, because this is where it begins; for how can we be at peace with the world if we cannot be at peace with those in the church? Yet how sad and how frustrating when it is easier to establish peace in the community than it is to establish peace in church! Jesus said, "Salt is good, but if it loses its saltiness, how can you make it salty again? Have salt in yourselves, and be at peace with each other" (Mark 9:50).

You can read the full story of the above feud in my second book 'The Cross and the Gun', which can be ordered via our web site www.newlifecitychurch.co.uk.

8

Ambassadors of Patience

Paul said, "As God's chosen people, holy and dearly
loved, clothe yourselves with compassion, kindness,
humility, gentleness and patience" (Col 2:12).

Let me remind you that in Galatians 5:22 Paul lists patience as
the fourth aspect of the Fruit of the Spirit. As ambassadors of
Christ we should be cultivating, growing and producing the
Fruit of the Spirit in our lives. Patience should therefore be one
of the remarkable qualities in the life of every true ambassador
of Christ.

Patience is something you should put on

Paul said, "Clothe yourselves with patience" (Col. 2:12). I think
it is enough to suggest that the Fruit of the Spirit does not come
naturally to anyone. This is perhaps more apparent when it
comes to patience, because patience is a quality that does not
come easy to any of us. Rather it is something that most of us

need to work hard at. We need to develop a spiritual work ethic so we can cultivate and produce this and other aspects of the Fruit of the Spirit in our lives. Paul said you need to clothe yourself with patience; you need to put it on, which suggests effort on our part.

Whatever you are wearing right now, in terms of clothing, did not just appear on your body. Your blouse, your shirt, your shoes etc did not just suddenly appear. Maybe in the future this is how it will be, but the fact is you had to put on what you are presently wearing. You had to clothe yourself. So Paul is simply stating the fact that patience does not just appear on us because we are Christians, but is something we must put on.

Patience is not required in every aspect of life, but when it comes to making the right decisions at the right time; when it comes to responding to awkward situations that suddenly surround us; when it comes to dealing with unforeseen circumstances; and even when it comes to dealing with awkward people, we need to know that patience is at least part of our spiritual wardrobe and that we can put on what we need when required.

Patience is being willing to wait

An old Chinese proverb says, "He who hurries cannot walk with dignity". I would add to this, "He who runs impatiently cannot walk with destiny". I have often heard it said 'you need to be careful you do not run ahead of God'. However, I do not believe it is possible for anyone of us to run ahead of God. None of us are that fast that we could ever outrun God! Yet it is possible to run ahead of destiny, but the person who does so inevitably runs into the wall of disaster. When they do, they not only mess up for themselves, but they mess up for those who run with them.

At this point I have to admit that I am not the most qualified person to write or speak on the subject of patience. I know several people who are seldom fazed by those things that often drive me crazy. They have such patience they can drive their car at 20 MPH on the fast lane of a motorway. They do so with the knowledge that a line of motorists are crawling behind them, all longing to pass, and all running out of their patience faster than they are driving. As everyone behind begins to let Michael 'Snailmacker' know what they think by honking their horns and by flashing their lights, the patient crawler is not fazed, but simply keeps on at a snail's pace as if they were driving Miss Daisy on a day out to Brighton.

I have to admit, I would be one those expressing my non-road-rage feelings from behind. So the fact is there are those who would be better qualified than me to write or to speak on the subject of patience. However, I am a preacher and a writer, and sometimes preachers and writers have to bite the bullet and preach and write in season and out of season. That is when we feel like it and when we don't and, when the subject matter suits or when it doesn't. We just keep on preaching and we keep on writing. However, the kind of patience I am referring to in this chapter is a lot more than just being content to sit behind someone who is driving their car slower than the slow boat to China.

It is the kind of patience that keeps you in the father's house until it is your time and the right time to take hold of the inheritance. It is the kind of patience that keeps you sitting in the field looking after the sheep until it is your time and your turn to sit on the throne. The problem is there are some, who like the Prodigal Son and like the band Queen, "want it all and want it now", but if only they could listen to the advice of Paul in Col. 2 who said, "Clothe yourselves with patience" or even to the advice of 'Take That' who sang "Just try and have a little patience".

David could have killed King Saul and could have taken the throne of Israel much earlier. Others who were 'backing him' were pushing and encouraging him to do so, to kill Saul and take the throne, but David clothed himself with patience and showed a willingness to wait until the right time; the time ordained and appointed by God. So even though he had been anointed by Samuel and even though he had the support of the people, David returned to the fields to look after his father's sheep and patiently waited until the right time had come.

Patience is being slow to anger

To say that someone is patient does not mean they do not get angry. It means they are slow to anger. It also means that when they do get angry they do so for the right reason and that even then they were slow in getting there. So once again we need to understand that we are referring to a higher form of patience than the natural patience of the world that enables someone to drive at 20 MPH when the speed limit permits 70. I am not advocating speeding, but I am making the point that Christian patience means much than a leisurely drive.

The fact is if it's Christian it ought to be better. Christian love is a higher form of love than the natural love of the world. Christian joy is a higher form of joy than anything experienced in the world. Christian peace is a higher form of peace than the human peace that depends on the absence of conflict. Christian patience is a higher form of patience than the natural patience of the world.

This is because Christian patience is the Fruit of the Spirit. It enables the ambassador of Christ to wait on God's time. To wait on God for God-appointed opportunities. To wait on God to open doors rather than trying to force them open. It also enables them to be slow to anger.

The fact is God has every justifiable reason to be angry, but he is always slow to anger. Moses, Nehemiah, David, Joel, Jonah and Nahum all said "God is slow to anger". Some of them went on to say that he abounds in love and in faithfulness. However, this does not mean he will let the guilty go unpunished. Peter said, "The Lord is not slow in keeping his promise as some understand slowness. He is patient with you, not wanting anyone to perish, but everyone to come to repentance" (2 Peter 3:9). The fact is God is patient. He is slow to anger. Yet when he does get angry, believe me, you do not want to be on the receiving end.

I remember while driving along a road in Texas reading several huge bill boards brandishing statements purported to come from God. One of these had the words, "Don't make me come down there", God. Although it was fun to read it did have a serious side to it, because it was saying that no matter how much God loves the world he does get angry with the world, but only because the world gives him reason. Paul said, "Be angry, but sin not" (Eph. 4:26). The fact is we sin when we get angry for the wrong reason. We also sin when anger comes too easy as our first response to situations and to people we have issues with.

If you want to get angry, get angry at the devil. He is the thief who "comes to steal, kill and destroy" (John 10:10). Get angry at the drug dealers who turn young people into helpless addicts. Get angry at the child abusers who victimise the innocent and the unsuspecting. Get angry at the dictators who imprison nations and persecute those who dare to speak out and stand against them. Get angry at the terrorists who are willing to brutalise, destroy and kill the innocents for the sake of a cause they believe to be of more value than life itself.

Get angry at the right people for the right reason, but do not get angry with those in the household of faith; do not get angry with other Christians just because they might not be at the same level you think you're at or whose theology does not fit with yours. Be patient with each other; be patient with your wife; be patient with your husband; be patient with your children; be patient with other people's children; be patient with the leaders in your church; and if you are a leader, be patient with your people. If you are a team leader in your church, be patient with those on your team. The reality is that no matter how much it seems like people are not pulling their weight; most people are trying their best and want to do better.

However, I fully understand there are some who have no interest in pulling their weight and working in fellowship with other Christians. I fully understand that some continue to harbour bitterness and hatred (yes hatred) in their hearts towards others, even within the household of faith. I know, for I have seen it. I have seen people join together around the Lord's Table with hatred in their hearts for those they join with. Such people need to be confronted and challenged. The patience in their case is to bring them to repentance.

The fact is, as patience is the fourth aspect of the Fruit of the Spirit, patience should be evident in the lives of those who are ambassadors of Christ. You might think you are the most impatient person in your church. You might think that no matter how hard you try you cannot improve. You might think you can never be an ambassador of patience, but God, through Paul, says you can. He says you can put on patience; you can clothe yourself with patience.

I remember one of those times when Kathleen and I were having some serious words with each other (her fault of course). We were in full swing when someone came to the door. The walls were almost vibrating and we were about to throw missiles at each other, but the moment the door bell sounded we immediately changed. I opened the door and with my best reverend voice I said, "Ah hello there Billy. How are you doing? Come on in." I then lovingly shouted, "Hey Kathleen! Look who's here. It's Billy. Put the kettle on!" At one point it seemed like we were heading out of control, but within a moment we were taking control of our feelings, our words and our actions, and all because someone rang the bell.

I am certain that some of you who are reading this right now can identify with this. You remember a moment, or moments, in your life when even though you thought you could not control your temper, you did. For some reason you immediately switched from the voice of thunder to something a little more angelic or princess-like. You took control.

Solomon said, "A fool gives full vent to his anger, but a wise man keeps himself under control" (Prov.29:11). The fact is you can be in control and you ought to be in control as an ambassador of Christ. You can be in control by putting on or by clothing yourself with patience.

If the God we serve and represent is slow to anger, then we also ought to be slow to anger. On one occasion when certain people refused to listen to Jesus, the disciples (his ambassadors in training) lost their cool. They wanted to call down fire from heaven to destroy the ungrateful audience and their cities, but Jesus told them to simply shake the dust from off their feet and move on.

It is not for us to get angry because of the decisions of men, but as I said above get angry at the devil who is the destroyer of lives; the friend of none, but the enemy of all. However, it is our responsibility to walk patiently before God and leave the judgements to him. As the prophet Micah said, "He has showed you, O man, what is good. And what does the Lord require of you? To act justly and to love mercy and to walk humbly with your God" (Micah 6:8).

Patience can be developed

One sure way to develop patience is by the way you think. Solomon said, "As (a man) thinks in his heart, so is he" (Prov.23:7 NKJ). The apostle Paul said, "Finally, brothers, whatever is true, whatever is noble, whatever is right, whatever is pure, whatever is lovely, whatever is admirable--if anything is excellent or praiseworthy--think about such things" (Phil.4:8). Then in Romans Paul said, "Do not conform any longer to the pattern of this world, but be transformed by the renewing of your mind" (Rom.12:2).

The fact is the way you think will affect the way you live. The way you think will affect how you react and respond to different situations. Developing patience in your life is so important, but this is developed by the way you think. Someone coined the phrase, "Think about what you're thinking about". A great phrase indeed. 'I think' it might have been Joyce Myer.

Patience leads to harmony

Paul said, "May God, who gives this patience, help you live in complete harmony with each other – each with the attitude of Christ Jesus toward the other" (Rom.15:5). As ambassadors of Christ we should be ambassadors of patience leading to harmony within the church. A true ambassador will not be an influence of division, but will be an influence of harmony and unity.

If you desire to be a God-influence in your city then try a little patience. Be an ambassador of patience, and be an influence of harmony in the church. Some might say, "Well what about when someone has a go at me and causes offence?" Well Solomon makes another positive contribution by saying, "People with good sense restrain their anger; they earn esteem by overlooking wrongs" (Prov.19:11). Ambassadors of Christ have the wisdom to show patience and to overlook offence and by doing so they set an example of what Christ would do.

This was the attitude of Paul who said, "For that very reason I was shown mercy so that in me, the worst of sinners, Christ Jesus might display his unlimited patience as an example for those who would believe on him and receive eternal life" (1 Tim 1:16). As this is true in Paul, so in us Jesus wants to display his unlimited patience that we also might be examples to those who do not believe. As such we do not give offence, and neither do we take offence, because we are his ambassadors.

9

Ambassadors of Kindness

You, therefore, have no excuse, you who pass judgment on someone else, for at whatever point you judge the other, you are condemning yourself, because you who pass judgment do the same things. Now we know that God's judgment against those who do such things is based on truth. So when you, a mere man, pass judgment on them and yet do the same things, do you think you will escape God's judgment? Or do you show contempt for the riches of his kindness, tolerance and patience, not realizing that God's kindness leads you toward repentance? (Rom. 2:1-4).

The first thing we need to understand is that kindness is not a feeling, but an action. Just like Christian love has nothing to do with how you feel about someone, but has everything to do with what you are prepared to do for someone – that you are committed to seeking their highest good. So the type of kindness demonstrated by the Ambassador of Christ is more than just a feeling, it is kindness in action.

It has often been said that a person can be 'kind hearted', but what does this mean? I would suggest that being kind hearted has nothing to do with being sympathetic. It is not about internal feelings of goodness directed at people or at animals, but kindness is about acting for the good of others whether they deserve it or not.

One morning in 1991 Kathleen and I were having breakfast while watching the early morning news. The BBC was running a series of special reports from Albania. We watched as images of children's hospitals and orphanages appeared on our television screen. The children had nothing. Most of them were naked with not even a blanket to put over them while in bed. It was also quite apparent that most had not had a proper meal for several weeks.

As we watched the sad images that reflected despair we found it difficult to finish breakfast. Kathleen actually began to cry. Through her tears and sobs she complained about the tragic conditions faced by these children in Albania. She then went on to include the apathetic attitude of world governments, including the United Kingdom, toward the plight of these children.

It was as though Kathleen was giving it to everyone for either allowing these conditions to exist or for remaining passive while children were literally dying of starvation or freezing to death. It seemed she had reached what Bill Hybles would call her 'Popeye moment', but then so too did I, albeit for a different reason! As I listened to her justified complaints I got to the point where I could 'stands it no more'. So I finally took a deep breath and said, "Kathleen! Stop your crying and do something about it". And you know what? She did!

She just went and took two '40 ton containers' to Albania loaded with supplies including food, clothes, medical supplies and blankets etc. This was not just being kind hearted, but this was kindness in action. So when Kathleen and six other volunteers went to Albania, they went in the role of ambassadors of Christian kindness. They recognized it was not enough to just sit there and watch television as it showed such pathetic images of hurting children, even if they were prepared to show some emotion and shed a few tears. But they got up and did something. The fact is that's what Jesus would have done.

At this point I would like to pay tribute to Kathleen and to those who travelled with her from Belfast to Albania. To the drivers, Stephen Robinson, Stephen Matthews, Cameron Crawford, and Brian Ward, and also to two girls who helped pull it all together, Carolyn McComb (now Dawson), and Linda Martin. However, I want to pay a special tribute to Linda who was my Personal Assistant at that time, but who later died in very tragic circumstances. This book is dedicated to Linda's memory for her act of kindness to the children of Albania. We continue to remember and pray for her husband Stephen and their three sons, Stephen, Colin and Scott. Their loss is our loss.

The Gospels are filled with stories that reveal the kindness of Jesus in action. Time and again it is recorded how Jesus showed amazing acts of kindness to those in need. He healed the sick; he fed 5,000 hungry men along with their hungry wives and their hungry children. He set people free from the demons in their lives. He raised people from the dead. He saw a woman who had lost her husband walk behind the coffin of her only son and in an act of kindness he touched the coffin and raised the woman's son back to life.

He even showed acts of kindness to those who were not necessarily in any great need. For example, at a wedding in Cana of Galilee he turned water into wine. The people were not dying of thirst. They were not in despair because the wine had run out. They were not in dire need. This was not a life or death situation, yet Jesus in an act of kindness turned water into wine so that the host would not be embarrassed due to the lack of supplies. This story has occupied the minds of many to this very day for one reason or another. But for me it demonstrates the fact that kindness is not just a feeling, but is an action that blesses someone whether there is an existing need or not.

Kindness can also be the withholding of action

I am reminded of the story of Lot (who spoke with angels) and how he said to the angels in Gen.19:19 "you have shown kindness to me in sparing my life". Lot had separated from his uncle Abraham who had provided for him, mentored him, and had been such a positive influence in his life. Yet, for all that, the Bible records that when Lot left Abraham he pitched his tent towards Sodom, a city that even then was synonymous with the worst forms of sexual perversion and abuse. Yet, as if that were not dangerous enough, both for his family and for others in his care, the Bible also records that Lot and his family was soon living in Sodom.

However, when God sent angels to destroy the great metropolis of Sodom and Gomorrah, the first thing they did was to take Lot and his family out of Sodom. Unfortunately Lot's wife died on leaving the city, because she did not follow the instructions given by the angels. Yet Lot knew that he, as well as his two daughters could have been destroyed along with the cities. The fact is his life, and that of his daughters, had been spared. It was for this reason he said to the angel "you have shown kindness to me in sparing my life". You can read the entire story of Lot in Genesis chapters 13 to 19.

So kindness is not only an act of giving, whether deserved or undeserved, but it can also be an act of withholding. This is where the words 'grace' and 'mercy' come in, because grace is giving something that is undeserved, whereas mercy is withholding something that is deserved. Grace is giving forgiveness, whereas mercy is withholding judgment.

The grace of God is that through faith we have received forgiveness and eternal salvation that is underserved (see Eph. 2:8), but the mercy of God is that we are no longer under judgment. Paul said, "Therefore, there is now no condemnation for those who are in Christ Jesus, because through Christ Jesus the law of the Spirit of life set me free from the law of sin and death" (Rom.8:1-2).

God has shown his kindness toward us by grace and by mercy. By grace he has given us what we do not deserve, which is forgiveness and eternal life, and by mercy he is withholding what we do deserve, which is judgment. This is why Peter said that God is "not wanting anyone to perish, but everyone to come to repentance" (2 Peter 3:9).

Therefore, as Christians, we are where we are because of the kindness of God. It is the kindness of God that has led us to repentance. The fact is God could have left us in our sin, but in an incredible act of kindness he has not only shown his love for us, but in that same act of kindness he has led us to the cross where mercy and judgment meet.

Paul said, "But because of his great love for us, God, who is rich in mercy, made us alive with Christ even when we were dead in transgressions--it is by grace you have been saved. And God raised us up with Christ and seated us with him in the heavenly realms in Christ Jesus, in order that in the coming ages he might show the incomparable riches of his grace, expressed in his *kindness* (italics mine) to us in Christ Jesus" (Eph. 2:4-7).

His love, mercy, grace, and forgiveness, the life we have in Christ, our present position with Christ, and our future hope in Christ are all expressions of his kindness. These acts of kindness are all expressed in and are experienced through Christ Jesus. Therefore, as ambassadors of Christ, it is incumbent upon us to so represent him that those same acts of kindness are expressed through us.

Even the act of giving someone a cup of water in the name of Jesus is an act of kindness on his behalf that will not go unnoticed and neither will it go unrewarded. Jesus said, "I tell you the truth, anyone who gives you a cup of water in my name because you belong to Christ will certainly not lose his reward" (Mark 9:41).

The filling of shoe boxes with toiletries or sweets to bless others; the filling of missionary boxes with cash to support those in other countries; the filling of containers that could bless hundreds, if not thousands; the digging of wells for fresh water in India; the building of churches and hospitals and schools in Africa; the purchase of vehicles for those in need of transport; the purchase of pigs and goats to support poor families; the going into all the world as representatives of Christ, beginning in the local community to the ends of the earth, are all acts of kindness on behalf of Christ, and those who do such things are his ambassadors of kindness.

Kindness can sometimes seem harsh

How often have you heard it said, "Sometimes you gotta be cruel to be kind"? Well, I don't know about being cruel; in fact I do know! I fully understand what is meant by the statement. But being cruel is definitely not the way to show kindness. I suppose the comment should be, "Sometimes you gotta be harsh or stern to be kind"! Being harsh or stern can sometimes appear to be cruel, but is not necessarily so. To be harsh or stern is to be willing to do what's right or to say what's right, even if what's being done or what's being said is hard to take and causes pain, but the objective is not to inflict pain.

It is not always easy to speak the truth with people, especially when you know the truth might hurt, but kindness is not shown by withholding the truth. Kindness is speaking the truth in the hope that it will accomplish a positive outcome. For example, if someone had BO and it was turning others away from them, and you knew it, ignoring the problem would not be an act of kindness. On the contrary, an act of kindness would require confronting the issue by speaking gently to the person concerned and simply and lovingly telling the truth. Go ahead, try it! You're thinking of someone right now; aren't you?

But more seriously, if there is an issue between you and someone in the church, the act of kindness is not to ignore it in the hope it goes away. The kindness is in acknowledging that there is a problem but instead of confronting the person, address the issue, in the hope that the spoken truth will resolve the difficulty.

Ambassadors of Christ will not shirk from their responsibility to do and to say what is right. They will rise to the challenge and will be ambassadors of kindness when they have opportunity. They will perform acts of kindness whether or not the recipient deserves it.

10

Ambassadors of Goodness

...we constantly pray for you, that our God may count you worthy of his calling, and that by his power he may fulfil every good purpose of yours and every act prompted by your faith (2 Thess. 1:11).

God is Good

This might sound a bit whacky, but stay with me. Paul had said in Galatians 5:22 that the fruit of the Spirit is, "Love, joy, peace, patience, kindness, (and) goodness". So goodness is the sixth aspect of the fruit of the Spirit and should therefore be evident in the life of every Christian. However, Paul also said, "There is no one who does good, not even one" (Rom. 3:12). So on the one hand, goodness should be evident in all of us as Christians, yet according to scripture, there is no one who does good!

What is happening here is that in Romans 3:12 Paul is using the term 'good' in the most perfect sense. He is saying there is none as good as God, because only God is perfectly good. Paul is not saying "there is no one who does good acts". He is not saying "there is no one who is good in character and in personality". He is simply saying "there is no one as good as God", because only God is perfectly good.

God is not good because he does good, but God does good because he is good. In fact this is the very nature of God. God is by His very nature good as He also is by nature, love. God is love, and God is good. He cannot be 'more good' than he already is, and therefore does not do good to make him 'more good'. The fact is God's goodness is perfect. Just as light shines, because that is what light does; and just as sound makes noise, because that is the nature of sound; so God loves, because God is love, and God does good, because God is intrinsically good.

We have all been told at several times in our lives to be good. The reason for this is that someone doubted our ability or our commitment to actually be good in practice. To be good usually means to behave oneself. We have also had to do good things in order to be considered good, because by nature we are, according to the Bible, deceitful and deceptively wicked. Being a good individual is something we all have to work at, except for God, because God is, by His very nature, good. There is never a time when God is not good, even in judgment, because his judgments are always correct and are always perfect. That is why Abraham said, "The judge of all the earth (will) do right" (Gen. 18:25).

The Goodness of God in Christ and in us

The fact that God is good means that Jesus is also good, because he and the Father are one in total unity. Jesus was approached by a man who said, "Good teacher, what must I do to inherit eternal life?" Jesus responded by saying, "Why do you call me good, no one is good – except God alone" (Mark 10:17-18). Jesus was not rejecting the designation good, but he wanted the man who asked the question to understand who it was he was speaking to; that he was in fact speaking to God.

In much the same way, Jesus never denied he was the Messiah, but wanted others to come to that understanding. It was for this reason he asked the disciples, "Who do you say I am?" Peter responded by saying, "You are the Christ, the Son of the living God", to which Jesus replied, "Blessed are you, Simon son of Jonah, for this was not revealed to you by man, but by my Father in heaven" (Matt.16:15-17). He never denied who he was, and he never denied he was good. So because God is good, Christ is good; and because we are ambassadors of Christ we are therefore ambassadors of the goodness of God, which should be evident in us and revealed through us.

So what exactly is this goodness? Well, I do not intend to give you a lesson in the Greek language, but it helps to point out that as there are several words in ancient Greek for love, there are likewise several words for goodness. The word used by Paul for goodness in Galatians 5:22 is agathosune (ag-ath-o-soo-nay) and is the same word used by Paul in 2 Thess. 1:11 where he wrote, "that by his power he (God) may fulfil every good (ag-ath-o) purpose of yours".

The goodness that Paul speaks of is not an inner feeling where you feel good about yourself or your circumstances, although there is nothing wrong with this; but the goodness Paul speaks of is 'goodness in action'. It is the 'Fruit of the Spirit goodness' where you live for a purpose and a cause that is good in the perfect sense, because it is a Godly purpose. You see, as God is the only one who is truly good then the only purposes that are truly good are the purposes of God.

There is no doubting the fact that there are lots of good causes within our world, and I am not suggesting we should not support them. However, we need to recognise them for what they are. They are merely good causes; e.g. Cancer Research; the Northern Ireland Hospice, and any other hospice; besides many other worthy causes, but the good purpose that Paul refers to is far greater, because he speaks of 'every good purpose of God' that have both temporal and eternal consequences.

Pursuing the goodness of God by pursuing the purposes of God enables us to say or to sing "I'm living for this cause, I lay down my life into your hands", or "Break my heart for what breaks yours, everything I am for your Kingdom's cause as I walk from earth into eternity" (Hillsong). These are not simply great sounding words to great music, but they are declarations from the hearts and lips of those who are not content to just sit there, but who desire to live as ambassadors of the goodness of God and who do so anywhere and whatever the cost.

Everyone who participates in good causes is to be commended, but only those who pursue the purposes of God will one day hear the words "Well done good and faithful servant", because only that which is done for Christ has an eternal reward. As someone said, "Only one life; will soon be past. Only what's done for Christ will last".

This is why it is so important that beyond all the good we do in this world we keep our eye on the eternal goal. Someone can be a good doctor and can add so much value to people's lives by helping to improve their health. Others can be good musicians, artists, writers, students, teachers, workers, husbands or wives, the list is endless, yet they can still miss the eternal goal. To be used in this world to save a life is an awesome thing, but to be used by God to help save a soul is eternally awesome.

Upright in heart and in life

The literal meaning of this particular word 'goodness' (agathosune) as used by Paul in Gal. 5:22 and in 2 Thess. 1:11 is 'uprightness of heart and life', which means we are to live for the purposes of God with hearts and lives that are upright before God and before men. Several times I have heard some say, "I don't care what people think about me". Well they should, as should we all, because what others think of us as ambassadors of Christ is what they will think of God.

The fact is when we fail to live and walk uprightly, our failure reflects on Christ. As a Pastor, known across our city and in other parts of the world, I know that the eyes of many are on me. That is not to say they are constantly thinking about Jack McKee. In fact they might rather not be. Nevertheless the moment my life and walk fails to be upright is the precise moment that many will think of Jack McKee. It is in that instant that I will lose all credibility and, what is worse, I will become an embarrassment to Christ rather than an ambassador of Christ.

When one very well known Pastor (I'll call him Pastor Joe) of a large church and an even larger ministry in the USA was caught out in a sinful lifestyle, people across the world began to talk about him openly and frequently. Even people who had not known him prior to this and had no interest in knowing him, the moment his failure was exposed, they began to talk as though they had known him for years. His downfall, at that time, was such an embarrassment to the church, to his family and also to the name of Jesus Christ.

Shortly after this exposure we were on our second visit to Israel when Kathleen almost got robbed by a Palestinian who was selling pictures of Jerusalem. I got into a bit of a dispute with him. At one point he said to me, "Are you Christian", to which with a sense of pride I replied, "Yes I am". He immediately replied, "Pastor Joe is a Christian and look what he did!" Wow! Even the Palestinians in Jerusalem were talking about him.

As ambassadors of Christ we are called to uprightness of heart and of life and to pursue the purposes of God. To pursue Godly causes; not simply good causes. Your every waking moment could be taken up with good causes and yet not necessarily be doing what God wants you to do. I might think it is a good thing to visit hospitals everyday of the week and to give words of comfort to as many patients as I could possibly meet within the parameters of a single day. Yet if that is not what God wants me to do then, despite doing a good thing, I will not necessarily be doing a Godly thing.

This is why many are frustrated in their jobs and even in their ministries. Not that there is anything wrong with what they do, but because many like Bono, "Still haven't found what they're looking for". Perhaps more to the point, they have not discovered the purpose of God for their lives. Many are still waiting for the prophet to ride into town in the hope he would speak a word over them. Even those who have had this experience are still waiting for it to happen as they console themselves with the knowledge that a thousand years is as a day to God.

It is only as you humbly submit yourself to God and as you pursue his purposes with an upright heart that you will truly discover your God appointed destiny and will enter into your God ordained inheritance. In the words of Paul who said, "I urge you, brothers, in view of God's mercy, to offer your bodies as living sacrifices, holy and pleasing to God--this is your spiritual act of worship. Do not conform any longer to the pattern of this world, but be transformed by the renewing of your mind. Then you will be able to test and approve what God's will is--his good, pleasing and perfect will" (Rom. 12:1, 2).

Ambassadors of Christ pursue God's will, because they know that God's will is good; God's will is pleasing; and God's will is perfect. However, it is not only good for them, but is good for all with whom they connect, because ambassadors of goodness know how to give it away.

11

Ambassadors of Faithfulness

*Now it is required that those who have been given a
trust must prove faithful (1 Cor. 4:2).*

Faithfulness is listed by Paul as the seventh aspect of the fruit of
the Spirit and is therefore something that should be evident in
the life and character of every believer and follower of Jesus
Christ. This faithfulness is more than a stance that one takes
regarding a theological position, but has more to do with
maintaining integrity in relationships.

The fact is there are those who are more concerned about
maintaining a doctrinal position or an elitist attitude than they
are about maintaining relationships within the Body of Christ. I
am not saying that doctrine is not important, of course it is, but
there are some who would not have fellowship with me if I were
to purchase a container of milk on a Sunday. Not that I do,
although I would if I needed to! But even that is enough for
some to break fellowship! I am simply using this to make a
point that some in the Body of Christ are more interested in

observing and imposing obscure laws than in maintaining relationships within the Body of Christ.

I can almost see them, just sitting there, in front of their television. There they sit watching with a critical eye and listening with a critical ear to every move and every word spoken by someone from a 'different camp' within the church. Then when they see or hear something that does not neatly fit into their golden ark they take on the alter ego of a modern day Pharisee, crusading against others within the church.

I was one of those condemned by 'fellow ministers' for going to the cinema to watch Mel Gibson's 'Passion of the Christ'. I am not certain whether the main sin was going to the cinema or watching the 'Passion of the Christ'. Perhaps it was both! Even more recently, we at New Life City Church were ridiculed for closing down our Sunday evening service for one night so that our people could attend the Franklin Graham Crusade in the Odyssey Arena in Belfast. Such an attitude, in my opinion, is much like that of the Pharisees who were more concerned about Jesus breaking their little religious laws than they were about getting to know Jesus.

So right off the bat I want to make the point that this faithfulness, as an aspect of the fruit of the Spirit, is more than a stance that someone takes regarding doctrine. It is more to do with maintaining integrity in relationships. The word that Paul used for faithfulness in Gal. 5 can also mean loyalty, reliability, trustworthiness, dependability, commitment, devotion and conformity. So an ambassador of Christ as an ambassador of faithfulness is someone who should be all of these. He should be loyal, reliable, trustworthy, dependable, committed, devoted, and willing to conform.

Faithfulness equals Loyalty and much more

An ambassador of faithfulness should be someone who is loyal in all of their relationships. A married man, for example, who is an ambassador of Christ, should be loyal to his wife. A married woman who is an ambassador of Christ should be loyal to her husband. Parents who are ambassadors of Christ should be loyal to their children, and children who are ambassadors of Christ should be loyal to their parents.

However, an ambassador of Christ should not only be loyal in family relationships, but should also be loyal in church relationships. They should be loyal to the leadership of the church whether or not they are part of that group although, more so if they are among those members that play a leadership role. Paul declared, "Obey your leaders and submit to their authority. They keep watch over you as men who must give an account. Obey them so that their work will be a joy, not a burden, for that would be of no advantage to you" (Heb.13:7).

This loyalty should not stop with the leadership of the church, but extend beyond to the entire membership of the church. The fact is we are of the same body. We are joined together as members of the body of Christ and as such we should be loyal to each other just as we expect our arms and legs to be loyal to our heads. What a mess we would be in if the various members of our bodies decided to do their own thing and failed to be loyal to each other. So likewise we expect each member of the body of Christ to be loyal to one another, but more so to the head, which is Christ. This same loyalty should be evident in all our relationships.

An ambassador of faithfulness should also be reliable. Faithfulness includes reliability to the point that, when you say you will do something, others know they can rely on your word. An ambassador of faithfulness should also be trustworthy to the point where others know for sure that if they shared their closest secret it is never going to be repeated by them. A good friend of mine often said, "I was told not to repeat this, so I'm only going to say it once"! My friend will be happy to know that I am not going to repeat his name in this book, but I will only mention it once (maybe later). An ambassador of Christ should be committed to faithfulness in all relationships. This faithfulness should include loyalty, reliability and trustworthiness.

Why not right now reflect on those significant relationships in your life and ask yourself how committed and how devoted you are to them. How committed and how devoted are you to your wife or your husband? How committed and how devoted are you to your children? How committed and how devoted are you to those in leadership within the church? How committed and how devoted are you to others within the church? How committed and how devoted are you to other relationships that might well be outside the church, but are important nonetheless?

An ambassador of faithfulness should be willing to conform when appropriate. This can only occur when we recognise that, whatever the nature of the relationship, it is not just about "me", but is about others. John the Baptist got it right when he said, "He must become greater, I must become less" (John 3:30), or as the NKJV puts it, "He must increase, but I must decrease".

Selfishness expects and demands others to change, but true faithfulness shows a willingness to conform in deference to others who play a significant role in our life. Jesus has already set the most amazing example of this principle as pointed out by Paul when he said, "Who, being in very nature God, (Jesus) did not consider equality with God something to be grasped, but made himself nothing, taking the very nature of a servant, being made in human likeness. And being found in appearance as a man, he humbled himself and became obedient to death-- even death on a cross!" (Phil. 2:6-8).

So this faithfulness is not about being faithful to self, i.e. looking after number one, but is about being faithful to others, particularly those important relationships in your life. First and foremost to God and then to those significant others in your life, and where you show by your lifestyle the kind of loyalty, reliability, trustworthiness, dependability, commitment, devotion and conformity that befits an ambassador of Christ.

The Faithfulness of God

As God is love and as God is good, he is also faithful. God is never disloyal. He is never unreliable; he is never untrustworthy; and he never makes promises that remain unfulfilled. When he finds vessels of faithfulness through whom he can demonstrate his faithfulness, then the body of Christ, the church, is built up, not on the false promises of men, but on the fulfilled promises of God who is always faithful.

God himself had declared through Moses, "Know therefore that the Lord your God is God; he is the faithful God, keeping his covenant of love" (Deut. 7:9). The God we serve is the covenant-keeping God. He is the God who keeps his word. He is the God who keeps his promises because he is the faithful God, and he expects and rightly demands that his ambassadors do the same. He declared through Moses, "he keeps his covenant of love to those who love him and keep his commands" (Deut. 7:9). David also declared, "All the ways of the Lord are loving and faithful for those who keep the demands of his covenant" (Psalm 25:10).

Those who fail to live according to the covenant of God by rejecting his word, and there are many who fall into this category today, will never know what it is to experience the love of God. On the contrary they will experience the judgment of God; not because God refuses to love them, but because they have refused to embrace the love of God and because God will always be faithful to his laws that are righteous and true.

The Faithfulness of Christ

As God is love, so Christ is love; as God is good, so Christ is good; and as God is faithful, so Christ is also faithful. He is spoken of in Revelation as "the faithful witness" (Rev. 1:5). He was faithful to the father in heaven. He was faithful to his followers. He was faithful to the needy. He was faithful to his mother even in his death when from the cross he gave instructions to John to care for his mother.

He was faithful in his ministry and was faithful to his calling. Not once did he misuse or abuse his position. Not once did he seek release from his commitment to the declared purposes of God. Not when he was being stoned nor when he was almost thrown over a cliff. Not in the agony of Gethsemane's garden and not even while hanging on a bloody cross when he could have called 10,000 times 10,000 angels to destroy the world and set him free. He knew it was not about him, but was about his faithfulness to the covenant of God and his faithfulness to us.

The Faithfulness of Christians

It is because God is faithful and because Christ is faithful that we are likewise called to be faithful. We are called to be ambassadors of Christ, and therefore ambassadors of faithfulness with the knowledge that God is making his appeal through us. Samuel was such an ambassador of faithfulness to the point that "the Lord let none of his words fall to the ground" (1 Sam. 3:19). Stephen was faithful to the point that he was prepared to lay down his life for Christ, as were others.

Paul understood the importance of faithfulness when he instructed children to obey and honour their parents. He taught slaves to obey and honour their masters. He taught masters to treat their slaves with the same honour and dignity. He taught husbands and wives to love and to honour each other as equals. He taught believers to honour those in leadership. Jesus taught us to love one another and even taught us to love and to pray for our enemies. This is all achievable, but only when we live as ambassadors of faithfulness.

Faithfulness in Ministry

As Jesus was faithful in his ministry, which included faithfulness to the father, faithfulness to the word of God, and faithfulness to his followers, so as ambassador of Christ we are expected to show the same faithfulness to God, to his word and to each other. The people I serve as pastor need to know they have a pastor who is faithful to them, but the pastor also needs to know that those same people, and including those who serve on the leadership with him, are just as faithful.

It is good to know there are gifted people in the church. It is good know that people can sing; lead worship; preach; head up departments; drive the mini bus; set up equipment; clean the church; work with children; work with men; work with women; work with young people, and so on, but over and above all of this the people need to know they have pastors who are faithful to them, and the pastors need to know they have people who are likewise faithful to them.

This was why David wanted to know when men came to join with him and to take sides with him against his enemies that not only did he have their swords, but that he also had their hearts. You need to know you have the hearts of your pastors and leaders, not just their ability to wield the sword of preaching and teaching, and that they are there for you when the stuff hits the fan, as it surely will. However, they also need to know that they not only have people who can play guitars and sing through microphones, and set up the platform, and drive buses, and lead departments, but they also need to know they have your heart, for therein is true faithfulness.

This was also why Paul looked for faithfulness as a necessary quality in others, and also in his own life. He referred to Epaphras as "a dear fellow servant and a faithful minister of Christ" (Col. 1:7). He referred to Tychicus as "a dear brother and a faithful minister in the Lord" (Col. 4:7). Then in writing to Timothy, Paul said, "I thank Christ Jesus our Lord, who has given me strength, that he considered me faithful, appointing me to his service" (1 Tim. 1:12), showing clearly that Paul understood the importance of faithfulness in all, and particularly in ministry.

The Relationship between Faithfulness and Love

There is a major connection between Christian faithfulness and Christian love. This was recognised by David when he wrote "Love and faithfulness meet together; righteousness and peace kiss each other" (Psalm 85:10). It is unfortunate that with such understanding he failed in the area of faithfulness and love in his own life, but at least his moral failure was followed by heart wrenching repentance. His son Solomon also recognised the connection between love and faithfulness when he said, "Let love and faithfulness never leave you" (Prov. 3:3).

However, we thank God that when we are faithless he remains faithful, for he cannot disown himself (see 2 Tim. 2:13). This is not suggesting we have licence to sin, but is simply highlighting the faithfulness of God even when we are faithless. To add to this Paul said, "No temptation has seized you except what is common to man. And God is faithful; he will not let you be tempted beyond what you can bear. But when you are tempted, he will also provide a way out so that you can stand up under it" (1 Cor. 10:13).

God presents us with daily opportunities to exercise faithfulness to and within the Body of Christ and to all with whom we relate in the daily circumstances of life. This demands correct and righteous decisions on our part that will enable us to do all we can do to maintain faithfulness in relationships regardless of the faithlessness of others. For "Surely goodness and love will follow me all the days of my life, and I will dwell in the house of the Lord forever" (Psalm 23:6).

12

Ambassadors of Gentleness

Always be prepared to give an answer to everyone who asks you to give the reason for the hope that you have. But do this with gentleness (1 Peter 3:15).

Have you ever found yourself in a situation where you have been questioned about your faith? When it seemed that your faith was being seriously challenged? When it seemed your faith was being attacked? Or perhaps someone genuinely wanted to know why you believe what you say you believe. It is at these times that you are not only presented with an opportunity to make a response, but you are also presented with a choice regarding the type of response. Your reply will either draw or repel those who question your faith, regardless of the reason. This is why Peter tells us that we should always be ready to give an answer and a reason for our hope, but to do so with gentleness.

Sadly there are many within the church, the body of Christ, who seem to think they carry a special anointing to question what everyone else is doing and to argue and debate for every and for any reason. We need to understand that it is possible to win an argument, yet lose a friendship. It is possible to win an argument, yet lose a friend. It is also possible to win an argument and lose a soul; at least lose our opportunity to lead that soul to Christ.

I remember watching a well known Christian politician who was being interviewed on secular television alongside someone who was gay. Both were from Belfast. The only thing the Christian politician was interested in achieving was convincing the person who was homosexual how much God abhorred him because of his lifestyle. The man explained that this was the kind of response he expected from a narrow minded Christian in Northern Ireland and further explained his belief that Jesus would have responded differently.

The whole debate degenerated into a live television debacle, and there was obviously no love lost between the two main antagonists as insult followed insult. There are some viewers who would have claimed that the Christian won the argument from a Biblical perspective, and they might well be correct, but he lost the opportunity to win a friend and perhaps a soul.

That is why Solomon said, "A gentle answer turns away wrath, but a harsh word stirs up anger" (Prov.15:1). The fact is the actions and the words of those who claim to be ambassadors of Christ should stand in contrast to the harshness of the judgemental religious attitudes of modern day Pharisees.

The Gentleness of Christ

I am reminded of the story in John chapter 8 when a woman was caught in an act of adultery. She was dragged by the religious Pharisees and thrown down at the feet of Jesus. They accused her of breaking the law and pointed out that the same law demanded she should be stoned to death. They were obviously correct in what they said, but they were failing to truly represent God, because God's desire is not to judge and condemn, but to express his love and to pour out his forgiveness.

In contrast to the condemnatory attitude of the religious Pharisees Jesus reached out with forgiveness summed up in his final words to the woman when he said, "Neither do I condemn you, go now and leave your life of sin" (John 8.11). Here the harshness of religion was confronted by the gentleness of the Son of God; not the weakness of Christ, but the meekness of Christ; for we need to understand that as gentleness is sometimes translated as meekness that meekness is not weakness.

Jesus Christ the Son of God was the embodiment of gentleness; he was the embodiment of meekness, but meekness is not weakness. He might well be the gentle Jesus meek and mild, but he is also the Lion of the tribe of Judah who will subdue and scatter all his enemies. He might well have spoken some of the greatest words of love and forgiveness, and he might well have instructed us to love our enemies, but when he needed to do so he called his enemies a bunch of vipers. He called them whitewashed tombs that were full of dead men's bones. He also called Herod a fox.

And although he gave himself and gave his life for the sins of the world, the Bible makes it clear that one day this same Jesus will judge the world for sin. Paul said, "For he has set a day when he will judge the world with justice by the man he has appointed. He has given proof of this to all men by raising him from the dead" (Acts 17:31).

The hands that touched the eyes of the blind and restored their sight; the hands that touched lepers and brought healing to their bodies; the hands that took the hand of a little girl who was dead and brought her back to life; were the same hands that turned over the tables of the money changers in the temple and took a whip to them and drove them out of the temple. These were the forerunners of the modern 'money chasers' in the church.

The gentleness of Christ was not a sign of weakness, but a sign of his willingness to yield to the eternal purposes of the father. Thus he set his face towards Jerusalem, and in total surrender to the purposes of God he walked as a lamb being led to the slaughter (see Isa. 53:7), and as God's supreme representative, Jesus, the messianic king, the Christ, the Messiah came in humility and in gentleness and fulfilled the words of the prophet Zechariah who said, "Rejoice greatly, O Daughter of Zion! Shout, Daughter of Jerusalem! See, your king comes to you, righteous and having salvation, gentle and riding on a donkey, on a colt, the foal of a donkey" (Zech. 9:9).

That king is none other than Jesus Christ the Son of the Living God who not only entered Jerusalem, "gentle and riding on a donkey" (Matt. 21:5), but who also said, "Take my yoke upon you and learn from me, for I am gentle and humble in heart, and you will find rest for your souls" (Matt. 11:29).

Gentleness of God

The gentleness of Christ is the gentleness of the father. For God is the supreme example of gentleness. He is often portrayed as a harsh judge, but God, the awesome creator, the giver and the preserver of life, is the God who also deals gently with his people. The prophet Isaiah said of God, "He tends his flock like a shepherd: He gathers the lambs in his arms and carries them close to his heart; he gently leads those that have young" (Isa. 40:11). When he speaks to us it is not with harshness, but with gentleness.

There is a great story in 1 Kings 19 when Elijah was told by God to go out and stand on the mountain and to wait for the Lord to manifest himself. Before Elijah got out and stood on the mountain a great and powerful wind tore the mountains apart and shattered the rocks before the Lord, but the Lord was not in the wind. Then we are told that after the wind there was an earthquake, but again the Lord was not in the earthquake; and then after the earthquake came a fire, but the Lord was not in the fire. After the fire there came a gentle whisper, and it was at that point that Elijah recognised the presence of God (see 1 Kings 19:11-13). God was not in the shaking, and God was not in the fire, but it was the gentleness of a whisper that brought the manifest presence of God. That is not to say that God is never in the shaking and that God is never in the fire, but that God is sometimes in the gentleness of a whisper.

Gentleness of believers

We need to understand that as God is gentle in his dealings with people, and as Christ was gentle in his dealings with people, so by his spirit he purposes to create and to cultivate that same quality in us his people, and he does so through the seventh aspect of the fruit of the Spirit, for "the fruit of the Spirit is love, joy, peace, patience, kindness, goodness, faithfulness and gentleness..." (Gal. 5:23). Paul also said, "Let your gentleness be evident to all" (Phil. 4:5).

However, let me again reaffirm that this gentleness is not an indication of weakness, for meekness is not weakness, but meekness is an indication of strength of character that enables a person, when their back is against the wall, to make calculated and proper responses both in what they do and in what they say. That same meekness will enable them to take hold of the promises of God. For even Jesus said, "Blessed are the meek, for they will inherit the earth" (Matt. 5:5).

We are to respond to each other with the same gentleness of Spirit that Christ the Son of God has shown unto us regardless of the fact that he knows us better even than those who are closest to us. For those men who are married, your wife thinks she knows you, but Jesus knows you better. Yet he still responds to you with gentleness.

For those women who are married, your husband thinks he knows you, but what husband can ever truly know his wife? Yet no matter how much your husband knows you, Jesus knows you better, and yet he still responds to you with gentleness. As ambassadors of Christ we are to respond to each other with the same gentleness of Christ regardless of what we know about each other.

Gentleness of Church Leaders

If believers are to show the same gentleness of Christ then those who are in leadership within the church should be setting the greatest example of that gentleness within the church. Paul said, "We were gentle among you, like a mother caring for her little children" (1 Thess. 2:7). In writing to the Corinthians, some of whom were complaining about him in his absence, Paul said, "What do you prefer, that I come to you with a whip, or in love and with a gentle spirit?" (1 Cor. 4:21).

Church leaders are instructed to be not violent but gentle toward those under their care; as seen by what Paul wrote to Timothy, a young Pastor, when he said that church leaders should not be "given to drunkenness, not violent but gentle, not quarrelsome, not a lover of money" (1 Tim. 3:3).

Later in the same letter Paul instructed young Timothy to "pursue gentleness", but he does so in the context of encouraging him to let go of earthly pursuits. As Pastor John Legge, my Associate Pastor, said about Zacchaeus, "he let go of his dignity and took hold of his destiny". I want to add to this and say that as Zacchaeus would never have taken hold of his destiny until he let go of his dignity, so you will not take hold of Godly pursuits until you let go of earthly pursuits.

This was the very context in which Paul instructed Timothy to pursue gentleness by letting go of earthly pursuits, which is to let go of those things that men naturally pursue. Paul said, "People who want to get rich fall into temptation and a trap and into many foolish and harmful desires that plunge men into ruin and destruction. For the love of money is a root of all kinds of evil. Some people, eager for money, have wandered from the faith and pierced themselves with many griefs. But you, man of God, flee from all this, and pursue righteousness, godliness, faith, love, endurance and gentleness" (1 Tim. 9-11).

Pursuing gentleness enables a leader to stay in touch with the daily realities of those in their care, but pursuing gentleness also enables the leader to stay in touch with his own realities and with his own weaknesses so that he does not think more highly of himself than he ought. As a consequence he is more able to deal gently with the weaknesses in others.

Therefore when the weaknesses in others become evident to those in leadership, they do not respond with a judgemental spirit, but they respond with the spirit of gentleness that reaches out with the desire to restore even those who are overtaken with sin. This is why Paul said, "If someone is caught in a sin, you who are spiritual should restore him gently" (Gal. 6:1).

Paul further instructed church leaders "Don't have anything to do with foolish and stupid arguments, because you know they produce quarrels. And the Lord's servant must not quarrel. Instead, he must be kind to everyone, able to teach, not resentful. Those who oppose him he must gently instruct, in the hope that God will grant them repentance leading them to a knowledge of the truth, and that they will come to their senses and escape from the trap of the devil, who has taken them captive to do his will" (2 Tim. 2: 23-26).

Every church leader faces opposition, and the greater the level of leadership the greater the level of opposition. TD Jakes said, "Every new level has a new devil". But our initial response to those who oppose us should be one of gentleness where we give every opportunity for healing and restoration, but always keeping in mind that meekness is not weakness.

I like what Paul said when he wrote to those in Corinth who were having a go at him in his absence. He said, "By the meekness and gentleness of Christ, I appeal to you--I, Paul, who am "timid" when face to face with you, but "bold" when away! I beg you that when I come I may not have to be as bold as I expect to be toward some people who think that we live by the standards of this world" (2 Cor. 10:1, 2). It is quite apparent that while he responded to his critics with some tough talk, his initial appeal to them was "by the meekness and gentleness of Christ".

Ambassadors of Christ are therefore not expected to respond to negative circumstances or to awkward people with an initial burst of anger, for such a response would only make matters worse. They are however expected to respond with the spirit of gentleness. It was for this reason that Jesus said, "You have heard that it was said, 'Eye for eye, and tooth for tooth.' But I tell you, Do not resist an evil person. If someone strikes you on the right cheek, turn to him the other also. And if someone wants to sue you and take your tunic, let him have your cloak as well. If someone forces you to go one mile, go with him two miles" (Matt. 5:38-41). Such a response would have saved lives during the Roman occupation of Israel, and such a response today could divert conflict and possible war, even in church!

13

Ambassadors of Self-Control

As Paul discoursed on righteousness, self-control and the judgment to come, Felix was afraid and said, "That's enough for now! You may leave. When I find it convenient, I will send for you" (Acts 24:25).

This is not the last regarding Ambassadors of Christ, but is the last of the fruit of the Spirit as listed by Paul in Gal. 5:22, 23. It is these that build Christian character, and it should not surprise us therefore that Paul should conclude with this aspect of the fruit of the Spirit. For if we are to be successful ambassadors of Christ we need to be successful in taking control of ourselves.

The phrase that Paul used when he spoke of self-control literally means to 'get a grip of your self'. It is the first thing you might scream at someone when they lose the plot and become hysterical. You yell at them, "Get a grip of yourself!" Perhaps you have had it screamed at you on some occasions?!

The problem is that most people are good at telling others to get a grip of themselves, but are not so good at taking control of their own lives. We expect others to be in control of their emotions and of their lifestyle, but are not so good when it comes to controlling our own emotions and our own lifestyle. However, there is an expectation upon all of us as ambassadors of Christ that we take control of our thoughts, our words and our actions, and that we bring our flesh into subjection of the spirit.

It should also be noted that the fruit of the Spirit stands in contrast to the works of the flesh as described by Paul in Gal. 5 where he said, "The acts of the sinful nature are obvious: sexual immorality, impurity and debauchery; idolatry and witchcraft; hatred, discord, jealousy, fits of rage, selfish ambition, dissensions, factions and envy; drunkenness, orgies, and the like" (Gal. 5:19-21).

In other words, anything that is self seeking and self centred, rather than God seeking and God centred, can be identified as the works of the flesh. For the works of the flesh to be manifest in your life you do not need self-control, you simply need to permit the fleshly desires to kick in and then just go with the flow.

For example, Adam did not need self-control to enable him eat of the forbidden fruit. On the contrary, he needed the self-control to enable him not to eat of the fruit. David did not need self-control to enable him to lust after Bathsheba; he needed self-control to enable him to resist the temptation. King Ahab did not need self-control to enable him to covet Naboth's vineyard; he needed self-control to enable him to walk away without coveting what was not his. You see, you do not need self control to enable you to sin; you need self-control to enable you not to sin. So when it comes to resisting the works of the flesh, as well as developing the fruit of the Spirit, you need self-control.

If you want to be successful as an ambassador of Christ you need to be in control of yourself; you need to be in control of your emotions; you need to be in control of the choices you make; you need to be in control of the things you do and the words you speak. Peter lists self-control as one of those qualities that will enable you to be effective and productive as a Christian. He further explains that without self-control you will become near sighted and blind and will even forget the fact that your past sins have been forgiven (see 2 Peter 1:5-9).

It was for this very reason that Paul instructed Titus to teach the older men to be self-controlled; to likewise teach the younger women to be self-controlled and pure; and to encourage the young men to be self-controlled (see Titus 2:2-6). It is my opinion that self-control is the most difficult aspect of the fruit of the Spirit, because it seems that all of the other aspects are dependent upon this one. Why? It is because we do not need self-control to exercise the works of the flesh, but we sure need self-control to enable us to resist the works of the flesh and to manifest the fruit of the Spirit.

I love the story about a teenage Christian girl who was being laughed at and mocked by her classmates because she refused to have sex with boys and because she was still a virgin. While some of them boasted about their exploits she finally stood up in the classroom, looked them all in the eye and said, "I can be just like you anytime I want, but you can never be like me". They might have had something she did not have at that time – sex! But this young woman had something they did not have – purity.

Self-control begins with the kind of integrity that recognises the following realities:

No one has mastered self-control

The first reality we need to recognise is that no one has fully mastered self-control. The question was asked "Who is fit to govern others?" The answer came; "He who governs himself". This brought the response, "You might as well have said, "nobody"" (Augustus William Hare and Julius Charles Hare, Guesses at Truth, by Two Brothers, 1827). The fact is there is no one who truly governs himself. So if the only person who is fit to govern others is the person who governs himself then no one is fit to govern others, for no one has fully mastered self-control.

This does not mean that self-control is unachievable; for God would not command us to commit to something that is beyond us. He commands us to love one another, because he knows we can do so. He commands us to make disciples of all nations, because he knows we can. And he commands us to pursue self-control, because he knows we can get there.

The need for self-discipline

The second reality we need to recognise is the need for self-discipline. This enables us to abstain from what is wrong and embrace what is right. It is the ability to abstain from the negative and commit to the positive. It is the ability to resist the works of the flesh and produce the fruit of the Spirit. It is the ability to live a balanced life not based on "Thou shalt not", but a life based on "This one thing I do". Self-discipline is not simply about not doing the things we should not be doing, but is more about getting up from the church pew and pursuing those things that are Christ-like and are worthy of his ambassadors.

Paul said, "I want to know Christ and the power of his resurrection and the fellowship of sharing in his sufferings, becoming like him in his death, and so, somehow, to attain to the resurrection from the dead. Not that I have already obtained all this, or have already been made perfect, but I press on to take hold of that for which Christ Jesus took hold of me. Brothers, I do not consider myself yet to have taken hold of it. But one thing I do: Forgetting what is behind and straining toward what is ahead, I press on toward the goal to win the prize for which God has called me heavenward in Christ Jesus" (Phil. 3:10-14).

This calls for self-discipline. It calls for setting structures within your life that will enable you to stay focused on your relationship with Christ. These should include prayer structures; Bible Study structures; fellowship structures; giving structures; faithfulness structures and so on. Life should not be haphazard. The things we do should not be disorganized. We need positive character building, life developing and life protecting structures. This is why Solomon said, "Like a city whose walls are broken down is a man who lacks self-control" (Pro. 25:28). Just as a city needs its structures and defences, so too do our lives.

The ability to control self

The third reality is that self-control is quite simply the ability to take control of self. It's not rocket science. As said previously self-control literally means to get a grip of yourself. It is the ability to control how you think. Not so much what you think, but what you do with what you think, i.e. what you do with your thoughts the moment they enter your head. The sin is not so much in what you think, but the sin is in what you do with those negative thoughts that are potentially sinful. Even Jesus had negative thoughts he needed to deal with.

He had thoughts of bowing to the devil, which were of course suggested to him by the devil himself, but he immediately dealt with those thoughts by telling the devil where to go. He had thoughts of turning stones into bread and of taking the easy way out, but he immediately spoke the Word of God over his life by declaring, "It is written" (Matt. 4:4). He had thoughts of dying in Gethsemane, but he totally surrendered himself to the will of the Father by saying, "Not what I will, but what you will" (Mark 14:36). So it's not the thoughts that are the problem, but it's what you do with those thoughts and how you deal with them.

I remember hearing a well known Pastor share at a Leadership Conference how that one day when his secretary walked into his office he did something he had not done before. He noticed how attractive she was and began to have inappropriate thoughts about her, but he immediately dismissed those thoughts. The following day the same thing happened, except on that day he did not immediately dismiss the inappropriate thoughts, but he facilitated them by permitting them to linger for a little while longer than the previous day. He shared with us that the sin was not in having the initial thoughts, but the sin was in facilitating those thoughts. However, he quickly took control and dealt appropriately with those particular thoughts by confiding with a close friend.

Controlling thoughts, actions and speech

Self-control is not only the ability to avoid negative thoughts, but is the ability to take control of those thoughts. Controlling your thoughts is the first step to controlling your actions. However, it does not necessarily follow that failure to take control of your thoughts will automatically lead to failure in your actions.

For example, you might have thoughts of wanting to kill someone. I sincerely hope not, but if you do, it does not mean you will actually do what you are thinking. For beyond your thoughts you can take control of your actions. An ambassador of Christ is someone who can take control of their thoughts and their actions.

Self-control is also the ability to take control of what you say and of how you say what you say. It is the ability to speak the truth and to do so in love. It is the ability to be accurate when reporting things like church attendance, salvations, and healings etc. It is the ability to not exaggerate when sharing personal testimonies or testimonies of events. It is the ability to speak with such integrity that what you say lines up with what you do. I have heard some preachers get to a point in their sermons where they have said, "I'm speaking the truth now, I'm not preaching"! Well the fact is we all want to believe that preachers are always speaking the truth, whether preaching or not!

14

Ambassadors of The Anointing

Jesus said, "The Spirit of the Lord is on me, because he has anointed me to preach good news to the poor. He has sent me to proclaim freedom for the prisoners and recovery of sight for the blind, to release the oppressed, to proclaim the year of the Lord's favour" (Luke 4:18).

The anointing refers to the presence of God on a person's life. So that someone who is anointed by the Spirit of God is someone who is a carrier of the presence of God. When Jesus declared that the Spirit of the Lord was upon him and had anointed him, he was declaring the fact that he was a carrier of the presence of God. Now we know that Jesus was more than just a carrier of God's presence. We know that he was the very embodiment of the presence of God. We know that he was in fact God with us; the eternal Son of the living God who lived and walked amongst us.

However, when he declared in such a manner that the anointing of the Lord was upon him he was declaring himself to be the Messiah, the Christ – the Anointed One. David prophesied about the coming Messiah when he declared, "The kings of the earth take their stand and the rulers gather together against the Lord and against his Anointed One" (Ps. 2:2). Daniel likewise prophesied about the coming Messiah when he said, "The Anointed One will be cut off and will have nothing" (see Daniel 9:26).

But the reason for the anointing of the Spirit of the Lord upon Christ was not only to identify him as the Messiah, but in his own words he declared that the Spirit of the Lord was upon him to anoint him to preach good news to the poor; to proclaim freedom for the prisoners and recovery of sight for the blind, to release the oppressed, and proclaim the year of the Lord's favour.

The anointing first and foremost was for the preaching of good news; the preaching of the Gospel. The greatest miracle is for someone to be saved, but the anointing is not only for the saving of the lost. The anointing is also for the breaking of poverty in people's lives. The anointing is for the setting free of those in bondage. The anointing is for the healing of the body and for deliverance from oppression.

The release of the anointing

My definition of the anointing is that it's the overflow of the presence of God and is released in various ways. The anointing that was on Jesus would bring healing and deliverance to people as he touched them or as they touched him. He brought healing to lepers, to the deaf and to the blind by simply touching them. However, sometimes the overflow of the presence of God was released through the spoken word. There was an occasion when Jesus was approached by a Roman Centurion who said, "Lord, I do not deserve to have you come under my roof. But just say the word, and my servant will be healed" (Matt. 8:8). Then Jesus said to the centurion, "Go! It will be done just as you believed it would." And his servant was healed at that very hour" (Matt. 8:13).

There were times when the anointing was released through contact with someone's shadow (Acts 5:15) or through the garment of Jesus (Matt.14:36). So why not a book? Some of you who are reading this right now need to know that the anointing of the Spirit of the Lord is being released upon you at this very moment. There is an overflow of the presence of God being released upon you to heal you from sickness and to set you free from whatever binds and controls you.

Even as I write I am praying for those who would read these words that the anointing to heal and to set free would be released upon each one. That even now as you read you will be healed and set free in Jesus' name. I pray for an overflow of the presence of God upon your life, upon your body, upon your family and upon your finances. Be blessed. Be healed. Be set free in Jesus' name.

The Prophetic Anointing

In the Old Testament the anointing was reserved for special offices and ministries. One of these was the prophetic office. Prophets were often those who were anointed with oil and were set apart for ministry. Elijah was instructed by God to anoint Elisha to succeed him as prophet (1 Kings 19:19). The anointing oil on the prophet was symbolic of the Spirit of God upon the life of the prophet and also within the ministry of the prophet. The prophet was anointed to speak on behalf of God, so that the prophet needed to be sure that what he said on God's behalf was truly from God. This is why I like what the Bible says about the prophet Samuel, for it clearly states that the Lord "let none of his words fall to the ground" (1 Sam. 3:19).

I am not into 'hit and miss' prophecies. I am not into 'give it a go' prophecies. I am only interested in hearing from those who are truly hearing from God, for only those who hear from God can speak for God. Only those who are truly led by the Spirit of God will speak words from God and will not speak words that will fall to the ground. Oh that God would cause a new generation of Samuels to rise up. Who would not only speak the Word of God with boldness, but would speak it with integrity.

I have no doubt that the ministry of the prophet exists within the church today and that besides these recognised ministries there are also those who would be used by God to exercise the gift of prophecy within the church, but who might not be recognised as 'ministering prophets'. However, the word prophet simply means a spokesperson. So that in simple terms, God's prophet is God's spokesperson.

A preacher is God's prophet, for he speaks on God's behalf just as Aaron was the prophet of Moses who spoke on his behalf. God said to Moses, "See, I have made you like God to Pharaoh, and your brother Aaron will be your prophet" (Exod. 7:1). Someone who testifies on God's behalf or who teaches the Word of God is speaking on God's behalf and is therefore a prophet of God. Sunday school teachers, youth pastors, worship leaders etc are prophets of the Most High God.

Prophecy comes in different ways. It can come through a sermon. It can come through a visiting speaker who speaks directly into the heart of the church or right into someone's life. It can come through study and through waiting upon God prior to standing before the people, or it can come spontaneously as you stand in front of the people of God. It can be written down or can be spoken as the Holy Spirit gives utterance. It can come through someone standing in church and declaring "Thus saith the Lord", but when they do so they need to be sure it truly is the Lord who saith it!

A prophet might be a foreteller in that he or she predicts or foretells future events as did John in Revelation. However, a prophet is more likely to be a forth-teller. That is one who tells forth, who speaks forth the Word of God. Not all believers will be foretellers, for not all believers have the same prophetic understanding, but all believers are called to be forth-tellers. That is to tell forth, or to speak forth the Word of God. This can be preaching, teaching, witnessing, singing or just plain old prophesying as in, 'The Lord is saying to this church…'

This is why Jesus said, "But you will receive power when the Holy Spirit (the anointing) comes on you; and you will be my witnesses (forth-tellers) in Jerusalem, and in all Judea and Samaria, and to the ends of the earth" (Acts 1:8). This is why ambassadors of Christ do not confine themselves to the four walls of a church building. They do not just sit there in the comfort zone of a church pew. Instead they recognize that nowhere in the Word of God is the world commanded to attend church, but that the church is commanded to go into the entire world to be the spokespersons of Christ who carry the anointing of the Holy Spirit to proclaim the Gospel and to declare the Word of God.

The Priestly Anointing

God told Moses to, "Dress Aaron in the sacred garments, anoint him and consecrate him so he may serve me as priest. Bring his sons and dress them in tunics. Anoint them just as you anointed their father, so they may serve me as priests" (Exod. 40:13-15).

The priest was someone who was called to stand before God on behalf of the people. The priest was the one person who could enter into the presence of God to bring with him a sacrifice for the sins of the people and to seek forgiveness on their behalf. The High Priest was the only person who could enter the Holy of Holies and to literally stand before God on behalf of the people's sins and the sins of the nation, but for this he needed the anointing of oil that represented the Holy Spirit. This was not a self-anointing or a self-appointed position, but came through a recognised leader. In Aaron's case he was anointed and appointed by Moses as directed by God.

However, Peter tells us that we are a "Royal Priesthood" (1 Pet. 2:9). The anointing for priesthood is no longer reserved for the few, but is now available to all believers. This is why Paul exhorts us to "approach the throne of grace with confidence" (Heb. 4:16), because we carry the same anointing that Aaron carried. This enables us to enter the presence of God without fear, but with boldness and with confidence. We come to him as sons and daughters, because Jesus taught us to pray "Our Father". However, we also come to him as ambassadors of the anointing, because we come to him as a Royal Priesthood to stand before God on behalf of others, e.g. our loved ones, our friends and our nation etc.

The Kingly Anointing

The first King of Israel was Saul, but only after he was anointed with oil by the prophet Samuel (1 Sam. 10:1). Once again the pouring of oil upon the head of Saul represented the Holy Spirit coming upon him to equip him for his role as king of Israel. From that moment every person who became king of Israel was to be anointed in the same manner.

However, as the New Testament teaches the priesthood of all believers, it also teaches the royalty of all believers. For we are not just priesthood; we are a royal priesthood (see 1 Pet. 2:9). John declared in Revelation that Christ has "made us kings and priests unto God" (Rev. 1:6 KJV). This is also why Paul tells us that "God raised us up with Christ and seated us with him in the heavenly realms in Christ Jesus" (Eph. 2:6).

The fact is we are seated alongside Christ who is the King of kings. This is not just our future position with Christ, but this is our present position with him. For Paul does not say we shall be, but that we are raised up with Christ and that we are seated with Christ. We are not just training for reigning, but we are in fact reigning with Christ today.

As Jesus is seated in the place of power and authority, so too are we. As Jesus is seated above principalities and powers, so too are we. As all things are under his feet so all things are under our feet. We have been raised with Christ and we have been seated with him as a kingdom of priests, a royal priesthood, alongside the King of kings.

This is part of the anointing. We are priests and kings in the Kingdom of God. There are no common people in God's Kingdom. There are no ordinary people in God's Kingdom. There might well be people who have titles relevant to their roles and ministries within the church. These titles might well get certain people into events earlier than others and might even secure a place for them on platforms, but these titles do not provide a privileged entrance or privileged places in the Kingdom of Heaven.

As ambassadors of the anointing we are called to stand before God as priests and are called to live among men as kings. Leonard Albert said, "Lord I do not want to be a millionaire, I just want to live like one". Well, we are kings who are seated alongside Christ and should therefore live as kings alongside men. We fail to live as kings when we permit circumstances to get the better of us. We fail to live as kings when we fail to represent Christ as his ambassadors.

Come on! Don't just sit and wallow in the mire of defeat and self-pity, but recognise who you are in Christ and begin to live as a king in the Kingdom of God ought to live.

Prophet, Priest and King

Jesus was the ultimate of all the prophets, priests and kings and was uniquely all three in one. He is the prophet through whom God speaks to us in these last days as clearly stated by Paul when he said, "In the past God spoke to our forefathers through the prophets at many times and in various ways, but in these last days he has spoken to us by his Son, whom he appointed heir of all things, and through whom he made the universe" (Heb. 1:1, 2).

He is the Great High Priest after the order of Melchizedek who has not only entered the presence of God on our behalf, but has also brought with him the blood of his personal sacrifice that was shed for us on the cross. Paul said, "When Christ came as high priest of the good things that are already here, he went through the greater and more perfect tabernacle that is not man-made, that is to say, not a part of this creation. He did not enter by means of the blood of goats and calves; but he entered the Most Holy Place once for all by his own blood, having obtained eternal redemption" (Heb. 9:11, 12).

Though he is the Son of God, he is the prophet through whom God speaks today, and he is our Great High Priest who perfectly represents us before the father, but he is also King. He is the Messiah King, the King of the Jews, but not only so for he is the King of Kings and Lord of Lords. He is the Christ; the Messiah; the Anointed One.

His anointing is ours

Here is the incredible thing. Jesus has passed his anointing on to us. Just as Elijah anointed Elisha to succeed him, Jesus has anointed us to succeed him by representing him as his ambassadors. Jesus declared, "All authority in heaven and on earth has been given to me. Therefore go and make disciples of all nations, baptizing them in the name of the Father and of the Son and of the Holy Spirit, and teaching them to obey everything I have commanded you. And surely I am with you always, to the very end of the age" (Matt. 28:18-20).

He also said, "And these signs will accompany those who believe: In my name they will drive out demons; they will speak in new tongues; they will pick up snakes with their hands; and when they drink deadly poison, it will not hurt them at all; they will place their hands on sick people, and they will get well" (Mark 16:17-18).

There is no suggestion in the Word of God that we have been called to be pew warmers or even to be church attendees once or twice a week. Yet many have chosen to just sit there, although they might stand from time to time to sing a hymn or two or even for forty five minutes of singing that might or might not be worship. We are ambassadors of anointing, and with that anointing we are to actively do the works of him who sent us. We are to actively impact our communities. We are to actively do What Jesus Would Do.

15

Ambassadors of Authority

Everyone must submit himself to the governing authorities, for there is no authority except that which God has established. The authorities that exist have been established by God. (Rom. 13:1).

"There is no authority except…God". God is the source of authority. He is its wellspring, its fountainhead. As God is the origin of creation, so he is also the origin and the author of authority. He spoke with authority and creation was birthed. He moved with authority upon the face of the deep and in so doing he brought order to an entire universe. Paul said, "By faith we understand that the universe was formed at God's command, so that what is seen was not made out of what was visible" (Heb.11:3).

Authority and Power

We need to understand that when the Bible speaks about authority it does so in the context of someone having the right to do something. For this reason we need to recognise there is a difference between authority and power. Authority is the right to do something, whereas power is the ability to do something. For example, someone might well have the power to enter your home and take what they want from it, but they might not have the authority to do so.

On 3rd March 2004 Kathleen and I went to bed at our normal times. She at 10 pm and I at 1 am! At 11 pm that night I had received a visit from a very well known Brigadier of a loyalist terrorist organisation. He had expressed some disappointment regarding public comments I had made about local taxi companies. I made it clear to him that I would stand over those comments.

At 3.30 am that morning Kathleen and I were wakened by the sound of breaking glass and what sounded like an explosion. It rapidly became apparent that our home was being attacked. I immediately jumped from the bed and called out to my son Jonathan, but he was already awake. Running downstairs, I foolishly turned off the alarm in case it awakened the neighbours! I opened the door and ran out to the front of the house. Thankfully, for them, they were gone!

My car was ablaze and completely destroyed. All of our windows on the first level were completely smashed and covered in paint, except for one that had a Liverpool FC logo on it. So right away I knew this was not done by Manchester United fans! However the point is, these men had the power to do what they did, but, Liverpool fans or not, they did not have the right to do what they did. They had no authority other than the command given to them by someone who had a twisted sense of authority over them.

Another example is that a police officer might have the authority to step in front of a car travelling at 40 MPH and signal to the driver to stop, but if the driver ignores him the police officer does not have the power to physically stop the car.

However, the officer might well be packing a firearm and if he has the authority to use it in that situation he might well also have the power to bring the car to a halt! So authority is the legitimate right to do something, whereas power is the ability to exercise that right.

More than a title or a position

Authority is not something you acquire simply on the basis of having a title or of being appointed to a certain position. Real authority is earned in a relationship of trust, and until that trust is established the only thing you have is a title or a position. You might well be a Pastor, and people might well respect the title, but they might not respect you. You might well be a leader in the church, and people might well respect the position you have as a leader, but they might not respect you, and will therefore not respect your authority.

Sometimes all you have is the title and the position, but you must make the most of what you have until such times as you build the trust where people recognise and respect the authority in you rather than the title or the position. When I graduated from Bible College I thought I had arrived when I got my first letter through the mail addressed to 'Pastor' Jack McKee. However, I was to learn through experience, often painful, that whatever authority I had was not so much in the title, but in my ability to relate with others and in knowing who I am in Christ.

But until you arrive at this point in your life and ministry you will need to operate under someone else's authority. For me it was the authority of the Elim Church. I still have that authority, but people now recognise that Jack McKee carries an authority that is more than that of his denomination.

Joshua first carried out his responsibilities and functioned as a leader in Israel by the authority conferred upon him by Moses. The Lord said to Moses, "Take Joshua son of Nun, a man in whom is the spirit, and lay your hand on him. Have him stand before Eleazar the priest and the entire assembly and commission him in their presence. Give him some of your authority so the whole Israelite community will obey him" (Num. 27:18-20).

For Joshua this was like being ordained by a denomination. Moses was like the Bishop or the Superintendent commissioning Joshua and conferring the authority of the Leadership of Israel upon him. This was quite sufficient to enable Joshua to function as a leader within Israel, but there would come a time when people would recognise the authority of Joshua as they did the authority of Moses. This took a little longer than having hands laid upon him, but involved a time of building relationships and building trust. The person who simply depends upon a title or a position to exercise authority over others is in danger of becoming a spiritual dictator.

Authority is relative to the person

The fact is some people can handle authority better than others and some can handle more authority than others. Moses said to the people, "Choose some wise, understanding and respected men from each of your tribes, and I will set them over you...... So I took the leading men of your tribes, wise and respected men, and appointed them to have authority over you--as commanders of thousands, of hundreds, of fifties and of tens and as tribal officials" (Dt 1:13-15).

It is okay to dream of bigger responsibilities and of larger crowds attending your church and of someday being a leader of hundreds rather than tens, and of thousands rather than hundreds. But you need to be doing the best with what you have and with where you are. You need to continue to faithfully sow seeds of growth through prayer and hard work. However, you also need to be sure that your hard work is God's work otherwise you'll just end up with a backache! The fact is hard work is not easy, and is especially more difficult if God is not in it!

But the point is you should not be trying to lead hundreds until you are able to lead tens. You should not be trying to lead thousands until you are able to lead hundreds. But then again regardless of the numbers you should be sure that whether it is tens, hundreds or even thousands, you lead with a God given authority that is recognised and respected by those you lead.

The moment a person has to say "I'm the boss around here" is the moment that he or she has lost the right to lead. The pastor or the church leader who leads from title or from position would be better off being a manager somewhere, because real authority, Christian authority, is never achieved until you reach a point where those you lead have given you permission to lead them. And the fact is people will not just follow someone with a title, but they will follow someone who has vision and has proven he is worth following.

Transferable Authority

As Moses transferred his authority to Joshua, and as Elijah transferred his authority to Elisha, so Jesus has likewise transferred his authority to the church and specifically to his ambassadors. Jesus gave authority to the disciples to drive evil spirits out of those who were possessed and to heal those who were diseased and sick. Matthew records that "He (Jesus) called his twelve disciples to him and gave them authority to drive out evil spirits and to heal every disease and sickness" (Matt.10:1). Mark likewise records that Jesus "Calling the Twelve to him, he sent them out two by two and gave them authority over evil spirits" (Mark 6:7; see also Luke 19:1).

Matthew also records that Jesus came to the disciples and said, "All authority in heaven and on earth has been given to me.

Therefore go and make disciples of all nations, baptizing them in the name of the Father and of the Son and of the Holy Spirit, and teaching them to obey everything I have commanded you. And surely I am with you always, to the very end of the age" (Matt. 28:18-20).

Someone said that whenever you see the word 'therefore' you need to find out what it's there-for! Well the fact is it always refers to the previous immediate comment, so that the 'therefore' in the above sentence is relating to what Jesus said about him possessing "All authority in heaven and on earth". With this he is simply stating that as he has all authority we can therefore go in that authority, because this same authority has been transferred to us, the church.

Here we see that the authority of Christ has been transferred to his ambassadors, his disciples, his followers, his church. However, it also needs to be said that he has never withdrawn this authority from the church. In fact he has sent the Holy Spirit to be the power behind that authority. He said, "You will receive power when the Holy Spirit comes upon you; and you will be my witnesses" (Acts 1:8). This partnership of Christ's authority and of the Spirit's power has been transferred to the church until "the very end of the age" (Matt. 28:20).

Authority to teach

Jesus "taught as one who had authority, and not as their teachers of the law" (Matt. 7:29). Teaching is one thing, but teaching with authority is something else. The church has many teachers, but not all teach with authority. There are those who teach because they know what the Bible says, but there are those who teach because they know what God is saying today. There are those who teach the written word, but there are those who teach the living word, which is the written word enlivened by the Spirit of God.

Don't misunderstand me; I am fully advocating that we teach the written Word of God, the Bible. This is the first essential of church life, but let's teach the Word of God not as the Pharisees taught it, but as Christ taught it, "as one having authority". The Word of God is "the sword of the Spirit" (Eph. 6:17) and is "living and active" (Heb. 4:12). Therefore, as ambassadors of Christ we should speak as those who have the authority of Christ and have the sword of the Spirit, and if the Word of God is living and active then we also should be living and active.

Authority to heal the sick

The centurion replied, "Lord, I do not deserve to have you come under my roof. But just say the word, and my servant will be healed. For I myself am a man under authority, with soldiers under me. I tell this one, 'Go,' and he goes; and that one, 'Come,' and he comes. I say to my servant, 'Do this,' and he does it" (Matt. 8:8-9). This Roman centurion understood authority, and he knew that Jesus had authority to heal the sick, even if they were at the point of death. Jesus was impressed and commended this man for his understanding and for his faith.

Sometime after this, as stated above, Jesus called his twelve disciples to him and gave them authority to drive out evil spirits and to heal every disease and sickness (see again Matt. 10:1). This was a transferable authority bestowed upon the disciples so they could go and lay hands on the sick so that they would be healed. He later said, "These signs will follow those who believe. In my name (by my authority) they will lay hands on the sick and they will be healed" (Mark 16).

Pastor John Lancaster, in his book 'In Spirit and in Truth' pointed out that when Peter and John were in prison the church began to pray for two things: 'power to preach the word with boldness and the confirmation of supernatural signs' (see Acts 4:23-31). Pastor Lancaster goes on to state the following:

'History has turned full circle….. But if the problem is the same, so are the resources to meet it. The authority of the name of Jesus has not diminished one iota, neither has the Word of God lost its power to thrust as a sharp two-edged sword into the hearts of men. The dynamic of the Holy Ghost is still available to the Church and the great supernatural gifts of the Spirit are still bestowed upon the church that will earnestly covet them'.

Authority to forgive sins

Jesus was challenged at every twist and turn by the religious Pharisees. It was no surprise that some of these men were nearby when he was speaking to a man who had been paralysed. Jesus told the man his sins were forgiven. The Pharisees immediately challenged him. But Jesus responded to them by saying, "So that you may know that the Son of Man has authority on earth to forgive sins..." he said to the paralytic, "Get up, take your mat and go home" (Matt. 9:6). The fact is Jesus had authority to heal, but he also had authority to forgive sins.

However, he also said to those who represented him, his disciples, his ambassadors, "If you forgive anyone his sins, they are forgiven; if you do not forgive them, they are not forgiven" (John 20:23). Now we fully understand that forgiveness only comes after repentance. This is an unchangeable Biblical principle. So Jesus is not saying we have the authority to forgive at will, but that we should be able to recognise true repentance and therefore declare true forgiveness.

Authority to overcome the enemy

Jesus said, "I have given you authority to trample on snakes and scorpions and to overcome all the power of the enemy; nothing will harm you" (Luke 10:19). While looking again at this verse for inclusion in this book I began to think for the first time that perhaps Jesus was not speaking about literally trampling on real snakes and real scorpions. The fact is the vast majority of people living on planet earth never see snakes, and the vast majority of those who do see snakes never see scorpions. Yet the comments of Jesus are relevant to all of us, but how can this be?

Well while most of us never see snakes and scorpions, we all have enemies. Jesus on some occasions referred to his enemies as snakes and vipers, and even referred to Herod as a fox (Matt 3:7; 12:24; 23:33). The enemies of the church are likewise snakes and scorpions. They have venom in their teeth and a poisonous sting in their tails, and their venom is becoming more potent in this end time generation. So Jesus is not sending us out to literally find snakes and scorpions so we can pick them up and trample on them, for the snakes and scorpions will find us, but he is giving us authority over our enemies.

Adrian Plass said that the phrase 'A close friend' is an anagram of 'a closer fiend'. Sometimes the enemy is at the gate. Sometimes the enemy is so close we might not even recognise him as the enemy. I remember when 'a close friend' and I were walking along a street outside Chicago. There was one point where a snake came right out of the grass and slithered across the path just inches in front of us and then slithered back into the grass. It made both of us stop dead in our tracks. However, the person beside me turned out to be a bigger snake than the one from the grass with venom in his mouth and a poisonous sting in his tail.

So when Jesus speaks about snakes and scorpions he is speaking about the enemies that rise up against us, but in the same sentence he makes the link by telling us he has given us authority to overcome all the power of the enemy. This is also why God said through the prophet Isaiah, "No weapon forged against you will prevail, and you will refute every tongue that accuses you. This is the heritage of the servants of the Lord, and this is their vindication from me" (Isa. 54:17).

This is not necessarily something we need to verbalise before it can be effective, but is something we live as ambassadors of Christ, for this is our heritage as servants of the Lord. For example, on a personal note, there have been several times when serious efforts were made to take my life. Besides these, several death sentences were formally approved by terrorist organisations in Belfast, whether it was a bomb under my car or armed men stalking me for three days and three nights, or with several shots being fired at me, or my home being attacked at 3.30 in the morning. Yet the hand of God has preserved me and the Lord continues to prepare a table before me in the presence of my enemies.

However, I am also acutely aware of the fact that many dear saints of God have been cut down in the prime of life and ministry. The first police officer to be shot dead during Northern Ireland's most recent troubles was a committed Christian. Several missionaries have made the ultimate sacrifice, including 9 Elim missionaries and their children who were massacred in Rhodesia (modern Zimbabwe) in June 1978, but with Paul we can all say, "For to me, to live is Christ and to die is gain" (Phil. 1:21).

Authority to defeat death

Jesus said, "I lay down my life--only to take it up again. No one takes it from me, but I lay it down of my own accord. I have authority to lay it down and authority to take it up again" (John 10:18). With this authority he raised Lazarus from dead even though he was in the tomb for four days and was already decaying. With this same authority he raised the daughter of Jairus from the dead. And with this authority he touched the coffin at the funeral procession of the widow of Nain's son and caused him to also rise from the dead.

With this same authority Peter raised Tabitha from the dead (Acts 9:40) and Paul raised Eutychus from the dead (Acts 20:9), because they took literally what Jesus said when he sent the disciples out and commissioned them to "go, preach this message: 'The kingdom of heaven is near.' Heal the sick, raise the dead, cleanse those who have leprosy, drive out demons" (Matt. 10:7, 8). As ambassadors of Christ we have been given authority to heal the sick, to raise the dead and to cast out demons.

Authority can be abused

God speaking through the prophet Jeremiah declared, "The prophets prophesy lies, the priests rule by their own authority, and my people love it this way" (Jer. 5:31). How sad when those who have been given such a privileged position of authority use it to so manipulate the people of God that even they are prepared to believe a lie. God's response to this abuse was to declare, "Their houses will be turned over to others, together with their fields and their wives, when I stretch out my hand against those who live in the land. From the least to the greatest, all are greedy for gain; prophets and priests alike, all practice deceit" (Jer.6:12, 13).

In an endeavour to ensure that authority would not be abused in the church, Jesus called the disciples together and said, "You know that the rulers of the Gentiles lord it over them, and their high officials exercise authority over them. Not so with you. Instead, whoever wants to become great among you must be your servant" (Matt. 20:25-26). Having authority in the church is not about lording it over others; it is not about manipulation; it is not about greed and deceit, but is about using that God-given authority to serve the church as true ambassadors of Christ.

I firmly believe that for the sake of organisational responsibilities and for the purpose of establishing accountability there needs to be clearly defined leadership structures within the church covering various levels of authority.

However, the authority given to us as ambassadors of Christ was not given to elevate some above others. The world's political and hierarchical systems should not be reflected in the church, because in the world of political intrigue authority is often abused, and if authority is abused then people become vulnerable to abuse.

Authority will always be challenged

I wonder how many preachers and teachers of God's Word have ever been publicly challenged while they are in full flight! In all my years of pastoral ministry I can remember three occasions when this happened. It actually happened twice in church. On one occasion a lady called out and said, in her Scottish accent, "Ach noo Pastor McKee. That's no the trewth yer teaching these people!" Then there was a second occasion when a young man got up off his seat and walked across the floor of the church and yelled at me, "What are you shouting for?" There was one other occasion that happened in the open air when it was not just words, but when snowballs were thrown at me. I understand, however, that others have experienced much worse than verbals and snowballs.

On one occasion when Jesus entered the temple courts he began to teach, as was his norm. The chief priests and the elders of the people approached him. They immediately began to challenge him. However, they did not challenge so much what he said but they challenged the authority by which he taught. They asked him, "By what authority are you doing these things? And who gave you this authority?" (Matt. 21:23).

The fact is when you exercise authority as an ambassador of Christ that authority will eventually be challenged. It is amazing where that challenge will come from. It will come from the modern day religious Pharisees. It will come from those who are jealous of your ministry. It will come from those who feel threatened by your success. It will come from those whose fire has gone out. It will come from those who aspire to be where you are. And it will come from those who just do not understand. However, regardless of the source of the challenge or the reason for the challenge, as ambassadors of Christ we must not fail to properly exercise the authority that is bestowed upon us by Christ.

Godly authority must be submitted to

Paul said, "Everyone must submit himself to the governing authorities, for there is no authority except that which God has established. The authorities that exist have been established by God. Consequently, he who rebels against the authority is rebelling against what God has instituted, and those who do so will bring judgment on themselves. For rulers hold no terror for those who do right, but for those who do wrong. Do you want to be free from fear of the one in authority? Then do what is right and he will commend you" (Rom.13:1-3).

Paul further said, "Obey your leaders and submit to their authority. They keep watch over you as men who must give an account. Obey them so that their work will be a joy, not a burden, for that would be of no advantage to you" (Heb.13:17).

This is why it is so important to be connected to a living vibrant denomination or to a fellowship of Christian churches where there is proper accountability. A Christian writer called John Donne (1572-1631) said, "No man is an island". It is my conviction that the same applies to the local church. No church is an island and should therefore not be isolated, but properly connected to the wider body of the church. This is not only essential for fellowship, but is prudent regarding oversight and accountability.

There are many negative comments being bandied around about denominations, and if we so desired we can all add to these comments. However, I have more concerns about those who choose to remain independent. Because those who make this choice often find themselves having to connect with others, but when they do so it is generally with those who are of the same kindred independent spirit as themselves. The end result is that they establish their own form of denomination but without the structure and accountability. The fact is we all need to be connected. We all need to have fellowship. But we all need to be accountable and submitted to authority. Even Jesus said, "Not as I will, but as you will" (Matt. 26:39).

So come on! Don't just sit there! As ambassadors of Christ we have been sent with the authority of Christ to represent who he is by being about our Father's business and by proclaiming the Word of God in power and in demonstration of the Holy Spirit. We have not been sent with a personal agenda or with an air ticket to take us city hopping around the world, but to so represent Christ that what we say and what we do on earth reflects heaven and reflects the purposes of God as revealed in his word.

16

Ambassadors of Power

But you will receive power when the Holy Spirit comes on you; and you will be my witnesses in Jerusalem, and in all Judea and Samaria, and to the ends of the earth. (Acts 1:8).

In the previous chapter we saw that the authority of Jesus Christ was transferred by him to his ambassadors. However, what we now need to understand is that with this authority comes also the power of Christ. Authority without power is an oxymoron. It's like having a driver's licence without a car; a gun licence without a gun; a dog licence without a dog, or a marriage licence without a wife! So Jesus has given us his authority, but with this authority comes also his power. This is part of the package and is so essential because without his power we can never function with his authority and could therefore never truly represent him as his ambassadors.

The power behind the authority

Every time a police officer walks the beat he does so knowing that he carries with him the authority of the law. His uniform and badge are symbols of that authority, but he also has the power to back up that authority. This power is represented by the gun in his belt and if that's not enough he can call for back up. Other police officers will come to his assistance, and again if that's not enough the army or the air force could be brought in! You see having authority is one thing, but having the power to back it up is another. It is the power that establishes and enforces the authority.

However, sometimes power is used to usurp authority. This happens when someone has power, but does not have the authority to exercise that power. It is one thing to have a licence to drive a car, yet not have a car. It is another thing to be in possession of a car, but not a have a licence to drive it. It is one thing to have a permit for a gun, yet not have a gun. It is another thing to be in possession of a gun, but not have a permit to carry it, never mind use it.

It was said by the historian John Emerich Edward Dalberg Acton (1834–1902) that "Power tends to corrupt, and absolute power corrupts absolutely". He went on to say, "Great men are almost always bad men". This is true in a world that believes in the survival of the fittest, where men can rise to the top politically only because they had the military might to put them where they are. But this should not be reflected in the church, yet I fear that all too often, what goes on in the world does actually go on in the church with a few hymns and a couple of sermons thrown in for good measure.

Dictators take their place and hold on to it, not because they have been given the authority through the ballot box, but because they have enough power to go against the democratic wishes of the people. This is evidenced in places like China where the ruling party maintains its position by its ability and willingness to use force against its own citizens. For example in 1989 there were the famous protests in Beijing during the month of June that led to the massacre of up to 3,000 people as reported by Chinese Student associations and the Chinese Red Cross.

One of the most memorable sights of those protests was the lone protester who stood in front of four Chinese military tanks in Tiananmen Square. He became known as the 'Tank Man'. However, several reports, including one major eye witness account, reveal that the 'Tank Man', 19 year old Wang Weilin, was soon arrested and was executed by firing squad, and all because he protested! Another book would not be sufficient to even outline, never mind document, the years of atrocities imposed upon the people of China by their own dictatorial leadership who hold a gun to the people's heads and oftentimes pull the trigger. But they do not possess a legitimate permit to do so. In other words they do not have legitimate authority, but only that which they have usurped because of the power behind them.

President of Zimbabwe, Robert Mugabe has the power to ensure he remains in office, but he does not have the legitimate authority. At least China does not claim to be a democracy, Zimbabwe does. Yet even there, in a so called democracy, power is abused to usurp authority. Like other dictators across the world, Robert Mugabe has the military might, the power, and also the willingness to do whatever it takes to remain in office against the will of the people.

Jesus said it should not be this way in the church. But "Not so with you" he said (Matt.20:26). He is the one who gives his ambassadors authority and also the power to back it up. We do not need to jockey for position. We do not need to get someone out so we can get in. We do not need to use our power, our own ability, to usurp someone else's authority. We do not need impose ourselves on any church. For if it is God's purpose he will establish us and will empower us.

God's Power

Because God is God he has the ultimate authority to do as he will, but because he is God he also has the universal power, the omnipotence, to back up his authority. Legitimate authority always has legitimate power. Whatever position a person has in life carries with it a certain level of authority; the higher the position, the greater the authority. But there is no one above Jehovah, the God of the Bible. For this reason God can do whatever he chooses. This was a lesson that was painfully learned by King Nebuchadnezzar who said of God, "He does as he pleases with the powers of heaven and the peoples of the earth. No one can hold back his hand or say to him: "What have you done?" (Dan. 4:35).

However, to have authority is one thing, but to have the power to back it up is another thing entirely. The Bible shows that not only does God have ultimate authority, but that he also has universal power. In other words he has all power, for he is the omnipotent God; the one with whom "all things are possible" (Matt.19:26); the one with whom "nothing is impossible" (Luke 1:37). With his creative power he brought creation into existence. With his life-giving power he breathed into a lifeless body of clay and it came to life as the first person to live on planet earth.

God's authority and power has always been challenged since time began. Almost on Day One the devil spoke to Eve and asked, "Did God really say?" (Gen. 3:1). This was a blatant challenge of God's authority. It is like saying 'Who does God think he is?' The devil went on to claim that even though God had decreed he would do something, it was never going to happen. God had declared, "You will surely die" (Gen. 2:17), but the devil said, "You will not surely die" (Gen. 3:4). So not only was he challenging God's authority, "Did God really say?" but he went on to challenge God's power to do what he said he would do by saying, "You will not surely die".

Well, both Adam and Eve were to learn to their cost that God did have authority over them and over creation. They were likewise to learn that God also had the power to exercise his authority and had the will to do so. The devil continues to this day to challenge God's authority and God's power. One of the greatest stories in the Bible that records an event when God's authority and power were put to the test is in 1 Kings 18 when Elijah took on the prophets of Baal.

Baal could do nothing. He had no authority and had no power. He was nothing but a man made image. But God, the God of Elijah, the God who is declared to be the only true and living God (Jer. 10:10), he is also the God who answers by fire; for though Baal could do nothing, God sent the fire to consume Elijah's sacrifice. God still sends the fire today. This is also why Jesus said, "You shall receive power when the Holy Spirit comes on you" (Acts 1:8). This is also why John the Baptist said, "I baptize you with water for repentance. But after me will come one who is more powerful than I, whose sandals I am not fit to carry. He will baptize you with the Holy Spirit and with fire" (Matt. 3:11).

God's Power in Others

The Old Testament is filled with those who were ambassadors of God's power. I want to mention just three of them here:

Gideon and the original 300

Gideon appears on the Biblical scene working in a winepress. However, he is not pressing grapes to make wine. O' no! He's threshing wheat! Now I might be from Ireland, but even I know that you do not thresh wheat in a winepress. We all know you press grapes in a winepress to make wine. So what was Gideon doing threshing wheat in a winepress? Well the Bible is quite kind to him in the story, because the Bible tells us that Gideon was hiding the wheat from the Midianites who had invaded Israel at that time. However, I am a bit more suspicious of Gideon's motives. I tend to think he was hiding himself from the Midiantes!

Anyway, while Gideon was threshing wheat we are told an angel of the Lord appeared to him. The angel called out to him and said, "The Lord is with you, mighty warrior" (Judges 6:12). Gideon must have been so startled. However, he chose to speak with the angel (just as well he's not living in today's world!). He then sought to explain how the angel had come to the wrong person (see Judges 6). Yet even after the angel had convinced Gideon that he was God's man of the hour he still had his doubts. He wanted to be absolutely certain this was God. So he put out a fleece to test the word of the angel.

Let me say at this point that there was nothing wrong with Gideon checking out the story of this angel. In fact it is strongly advisable that if an angel ever speaks to you and gives you direction that you check it out with God as best you can. We are told to test the spirits. John said, "Dear friends, do not believe every spirit, but test the spirits to see whether they are from God, because many false prophets have gone out into the world" (1 John 4:1). Paul also warned us when he said, "But even if we or an angel from heaven should preach a gospel other than the one we preached to you, let him be eternally condemned!" (Gal. 1:8). What a different world we would be living in today if Joseph Smith, and especially if Mohammad had tested the spirit of the angels who visited them!

So Gideon rightly tested the word of the angel. After the double fleece test, followed by additional confirmation that included a dream and a barley loaf, Gideon gathered 32,000 men to fight the Midianites. He must have been pleased with such an achievement to have amassed such an army, but then God went and spoiled the party by telling Gideon he did not need this size of an army. He was to reduce it. He did so to 22,000, but even that was too many. His army was finally reduced to 300 men. You see it was not about Gideon's ability to muster such an army. It was not about his strength or about their strength. But this was about God and about his power to work through Gideon with a handful of faithful men who would determine to remain in their place when it would be so much easier to run. This was about God's power at work within them.

Referring to human ability God declared, "Not by might nor by power, but by my spirit says the Lord Almighty" (Zech. 4:6). If God had permitted Gideon to use the 32,000 men then Gideon could have claimed credit for the victory, but with 300 it had to be God! Sometimes God permits us to be reduced so that when the miracle comes we would know that it did so by his power and not by our ability.

Samson and his jawbone

I don't mean Samson's own jawbone, but the jawbone of an ass that Samson carried around with him and used it quite effectively at times as a weapon against his enemies. He was obviously not the kind of guy to mess with. Yet the Philistines were often upsetting him and on one occasion he must have turned green and then ripped through his shirt before killing 1,000 of them using the jawbone of an ass as a weapon (Judges 15:16).

His strength was more than simple human strength, but was supernatural in its origin. His strength was not in his ability to wield a jawbone, nor was it due to the length of his hair, as some supposed, but his extraordinary strength was rooted in his obedience to God. Samson was a Nazarite who had vowed to separate himself from the world to devote himself to the service of God. One of his vows was that a knife would never come near his hair. His hair was to remain uncut as a sign of his obedience to God.

However, following the cunningness of Delilah, Samson was tricked into having his hair cut after which he lost his strength. He did not lose his strength because he had his hair cut, but he lost his strength because he broke his vows to God. His strength, his power, was in his willingness to walk in obedience to God who "gives strength to the weary and increases the power of the weak" (Isa. 40:29).

David and his slingshot

As a boy David had learned the skill of fending off the scavengers that would seek to steal and devour his father's sheep. However, his power was not only in his ability to use a sling and a stone, but in his willingness to serve God. When he later faced Goliath, in that epic confrontation recorded in 1 Sam. 17, he did so in the name of "the Lord Almighty, the God of the armies of Israel" (1 Sam. 17: 45). That is to say that David approached Goliath not because he had a slingshot and a few stones, but he did so with the authority and the power of God.

This truly is the story of the underdog, but the underdog was Goliath, not David. With the size of Goliath and with God on his side David could not miss. He took five stones for one reason only: so that preachers could speculate and spiritualise about the other four for the next 3,000 years, yet he only needed one. Goliath was the first of many, for David was to go on from strength to strength. Even to the point where the young women in Israel began to sing, "Saul has slain his thousands, and David his tens of thousands" (1 Sam. 18:7).

As ambassadors of God Gideon, Samson, David, and many like them, operated with God's authority and power. They had the right to do what they did and had the power, the ability, to see it through. This same authority and power has been transferred to every believer and follower of Christ today.

God's Power in the Church

The Church is the representative of Christ on the earth today. Not religion; not the prophets, but the church. It was to the first members of the early church that Jesus said, "You will receive power when the Holy Spirit comes on you" (Acts 1:8). He taught the disciples about the coming of the Holy Spirit who would lead, teach and empower the church. On another occasion Jesus breathed on the disciples and said "receive the Holy Spirit" (John 20:22), yet even after this experience he still told them to "stay in the city until you have been clothed with power from on high" (Luke 24:49). Even John the Baptist said, "He will baptise you with the Holy Spirit and with fire" (Matt. 3:11).

Jesus made it clear what this power is for. He said "you will be my witnesses" (Acts 1:8). First and foremost we are called to be witnesses of Christ and are empowered to do so by the Holy Spirit. This requires action and boldness. But it also requires that we get off our spiritual high chairs. Jesus is not looking to pack his church with spoon fed followers and with church crawling sermon tasters or experience seekers. He is looking to raise up those who will be strong in him and who will go everywhere proclaiming the Gospel in word and in deed.

This is underlined in a recent song by Tim Hughes entitled 'God of Justice' where he writes, "We must go, Live to feed the hungry, Stand beside the broken, We must go, Stepping forward, Keep us from just singing, Move us into action"[1]. The same is underlined by Casting Crowns in their song entitled 'If we are

1. God of Justice by Tim Hughes.Copyright © 2004 Thankyou Music

the body' where the chorus asks the question, "But if we are the Body, Why aren't His arms reaching, Why aren't His hands healing, Why aren't His words teaching, And if we are the Body, Why aren't His feet going, Why is His love not showing them there is a way".

Further to the above we need to understand that we have been empowered to overcome our enemies. In fact Jesus said that he has given us power "to overcome all the power of the enemy" (Luke 10:19). Paul in writing to Timothy said that God has given us a 'Spirit of power' (2 Tim. 1:7). Yet many still struggle with fear, with weaknesses, and with failure. But as ambassadors of Christ we have been given the power to overcome these negative character traits. However this does not mean we will not experience fear, or that we will not have weaknesses, or that we will not fail from time to time. But it means that rather than these defeating us, we have the power to rise above them and to live in freedom from their domination over us.

Power over fear, weaknesses, and failures

Fears that become phobias in our lives are never good for us. Yet there is such a thing as a healthy fear. It's the kind of fear that could someday save your life. There's an old story about two Irishmen who were on safari together in Africa. As they trekked through the jungle they were suddenly confronted by a lion standing in their path and looking menacingly at them. Patrick bent over and picked up a lump of wood and threw it at the lion hitting it right on the head. He immediately turned to his friend and screamed, "Run Seamus", to which Seamus replied, "Why should I run? It wasn't me who threw the wood!" He had no sense of fear and therefore no sense of reality.

I remember one night a man with a gun stepped out in front of me. He lifted it and pointed it straight at me. I had no time to think, but only seconds to respond. I did not respond by claiming my ambassadorial rights as a Christian. Neither did I rebuke the gunman in the name of Jesus (sorry for those reading this who might have thought more of me), but I very quickly turned and began running in the opposite direction. He fired five shots, and though I could hear every bullet being fired and could almost feel them passing me by, he missed with every shot. My fear that night was a healthy fear that saved my life.

The reason I survived was not that he was a lousy shot or that I was an excellent sprinter, because while he might well have been a lousy shot I was by no means an excellent sprinter, but the reason I survived was quite simply down to the fact that I ran. And I ran because of fear. However, I did not spend the rest of my life looking over my shoulder and living in fear of the man with the gun. I chose to rise above that kind of dominant fear and to live life with boldness as an ambassador of Christ.

Similar things have happened in subsequent years including a bomb being placed under my car; several death threats and actual attempts made on my life including another occasion when shots were fired in my direction as I stood speaking with a police officer. This happened in my home community shortly after I had finished church on a Sunday night. Once again the bullets came close. I could hear them whizzing past with some hitting a fence and a lamppost next to me and the police officer. Then there was that time when our home was attacked at 3.30 in the morning as recorded in the previous chapter. Yet even then I did not give in to fear. I experienced it! Of course I did! Of that there is no doubt, but I did not permit it to dominate me.

I am also happy to admit that like everyone else I have my own particular weaknesses. Two of these are chocolate and ice cream. The rest I will not go into! The fact is we all have weaknesses. However, these weaknesses, whatever they are, should not be the end of us; for even in our weaknesses we can know his strength. This is why Paul said "when I am weak, then

I am strong" (2 Cor. 12:10). It is also why Isaiah said, "He gives strength to the weary and increases the power of the weak" (Isa. 40:29).

As far as failures are concerned I would not be where I am today had it not been for the failures and the mistakes that I had made on the way to getting here. Life is a journey, as is success. And there can seldom be success in life without failure. The joy and excitement of achievement and breakthrough are seldom reached without the disappointment and pain of failure.

Ambassadors of Christ are not superhuman, but they live and they achieve by supernatural power. They experience fear, weakness and failure, but are not content to sit back and take their "ease in Zion" (Amos 6:1), but from the ashes of adversity they emerge as over comers, because they know that "greater is he that is in you, than he that is in the world" (1 John 4:4).

17

Ambassadors of the Cross

For Christ did not send me to baptize, but to preach the gospel--not with words of human wisdom, lest the cross of Christ be emptied of its power. For the message of the cross is foolishness to those who are perishing, but to us who are being saved it is the power of God. (1 Cor. 1:17, 18).

In the previous chapter we looked at the power of God in individuals and in the church. We looked at the power to heal and to set people free from their fears, weaknesses and failures. But in this final chapter I want you to see that it's the cross that is central to the Christian message. Without the cross, and of course without the resurrection, we have no message. Without the cross we are just another meaningless and powerless religion. It is the cross that gives significance and uniqueness to Christianity.

God's Master Plan

But who on earth could come up with the cross? No one! For the cross was not designed on earth, neither was it designed in hell, but the cross was designed in heaven. The fact is the cross was God's idea, not man's and certainly not the devil's idea. This was not the devil's blue print. This was not the devil's master plan, but the cross was God's master plan for the redemption of humanity and of the entire creation.

Before there was a sinner there was a saviour. Before there was a tree in Eden there was a cross prepared for Calvary; for Jesus is the lamb slain from before the foundation of the earth; that is before the earth was formed. For this reason we are told in Revelation that "all whose names have not been written in the book of life belonging to the Lamb that was slain from the creation of the world" (Rev. 13:8). This reveals that the crucifixion of Jesus was an accomplished fact in the mind of God long before it was ever an event on earth.

The fact is when it comes to the cross, it had to be God, for no one in their right mind would have dreamed up the cross as the emblem of their faith. Perhaps a sword or a throne, perhaps the sun or the moon, but not a cross. Well, a cross it is. It might well be foolishness to some and a stumbling block to others, but the cross is central to the Christian message and is the central cause for which we live as ambassadors of Christ.

Paul accepts that the message of the cross is foolishness to those who are lost and need help. He recognises that not everyone thinks of the cross in the same way as its ambassadors do. He knows that many see it as foolishness and have so turned against its message that they have become its enemies. It's what drove him to write, "I have often told you before and now say again even with tears, many live as enemies of the cross of Christ" (Phil. 3:18).

But why is the cross foolishness to anyone? And why specifically is it foolishness to those who are perishing? Well, in some respect it is understandable, because whenever you think of a deliverer you do not tend to think of someone on a cross, but you are more inclined to think of someone who leads his victorious forces against his enemies and ultimately crushes them. By so doing he becomes the liberator of those held captive by such an enemy.

Like David who led the Israelite forces against the might of the Philistine invaders. Beginning with Goliath he went forward to break the back of the Philistines and destroyed their hold over Israel. Then there was Alexander the Great who led the armies of Greece against the Medes and Persians bringing an end to their world dominance and establishing the might of the Greek Empire prior to the emergence of the Romans.

In the minds of those living at the beginning of the first century a deliverer was someone like David or Alexander the Great; a soldier; a warrior; a commander of an army with a proven victorious record. Therefore, for the early church to promote a crucified Jesus of Nazareth as a deliverer was nothing short of foolishness. He did not ride into the city on a white horse, but on the back of a borrowed donkey. He had never taken pole position at the front of an invading army. He had never fought on the battlefield against a raging enemy. He never defeated an opposing army. He never wielded a sword. He never fired a shot in anger or even in defence. He did none of these things.

But instead he preached sermons. He taught in parables. He turned water into wine at weddings. He fed the hungry. He healed the sick. He cleansed lepers. He raised people from the dead. He told his followers to love their enemies and to do good to those who hated them, and he seldom spoke a word in anger. He was beaten and brutalised. He finally carried a rough wooden cross through the streets of Jerusalem to a place of public execution. His broken bloodied body was nailed to the cross and then lifted up so that all would see his public humiliation.

Shortly after this his followers began to speak of him as saviour, the deliverer, but this, including claims of resurrection, did not compute in the first century mindset. Yet there were those who did believe. They believed because they had spent time with him. They had gotten to know him. They watched him live and they watched him die. They placed his lifeless broken and bloodied body inside a tomb, yet a few days later he stood before them as the living and victorious saviour who had defeated death. Having done so he now offers life abundant and life eternal to all who believe in him and who follow him. Therefore to be ambassadors of the cross is to represent God's master plan regardless of the fact that to many the cross is still foolishness.

Why the cross?

Why did God not send legions of angels to command people to repent? Why did he not write his message clearly across the skies for all to see and understand? Why did he not thunder his voice from the highest heavens to the ends of the earth that all would hear and be saved? Well the first thing we need to understand is that God does not do things as we would do them. God declared through the prophet Isaiah, "As the heavens are higher than the earth, so are my ways higher than your ways and my thoughts than your thoughts" (Isa. 55:9). So God does not think as we think and does not act as we act.

That's why God often tells people to do things that are beyond what seems to be normal to them. For example, when the Egyptian army was about to come down on the people of Israel whose advance had been blocked by the Red Sea, God told Moses to stretch forth the rod in his hand and to touch the sea with the rod. As Moses responded in obedience the sea opened before them and they crossed over on dry ground.

When Joshua led the people against Jericho everything in him was saying attack the city, but God told him to walk the people around the city walls for seven days. As Joshua responded in obedience the walls of Jericho came tumbling down and the city was captured. When Gideon mustered an army of 32,000 men God told him to reduce the number to 300. As Gideon responded in obedience God used those 300 men to secure an awesome victory over the Midianites. These examples help us understand that God does not think and act as we do and that he does not see things as we see them. So when it comes to the cross, the very thought of the cross brings confusion to the human mindset, not only of the first century but of the 21st century.

So the cross is foolishness to the natural mindset because it does not fit with the way we think. "Give me a sword". "Give me a throne". That's how we think! Not a cross! So it had to be God. However, more important is the fact that God chose the cross because there was no other way to set people free from sin and its effects. The angel Gabriel said to Joseph, "You are to call his name Jesus, for he will save his people from their sins" (Matt.1:21), but why the cross?

Well, because the cross was the only means by which Jesus the saviour could save his people from their sins. You see sin did two major things that needed to be reversed. It placed humanity under judgement of death and under a curse that ended its relationship with God. So the fact is for Jesus to become our deliverer he had to remove both the judgement and the curse, and he achieved this through the cross.

By dying on the cross he died our death and he took our curse. John Maxwell said, "Jesus did not come to put us in our place, but he came to put himself in our place". Another famous

John, as in Newton, said, "The Son of God became the Son of Man that we the sons of men might become the sons of God". The cross was the means of achieving this. No other form of death would have achieved what the cross did. That's why the devil tried to have Jesus killed by any other means.

He tried to have Jesus killed by stoning. He tried to have him killed by stirring up the mob to have him thrown over a cliff. He tried to have him killed in Gethsemane the night before the crucifixion. But no other method of death would accomplish his purposes as saviour. It may seem foolishness and even offensive to the natural mind, but it makes a lot of sense to God, because in dying, Christ was dying our death. In hanging on the cross he not only took our punishment by dying our death but he was made a curse on our behalf. As Paul quoting Moses said, "Cursed is everyone who hung on a tree" (Gal. 3:13; see also Deut. 21:23).

This is why the message of the cross is so central to what the Bible teaches, because there is no other way but the cross and there is no other person but Christ who declared, "I am the way, the truth and the life. No one comes to the father except through me" (John 14:6). So Paul declares that the cross is foolishness to some, but to those who believe "it is the power of God" (1 Cor. 1:18). Ambassadors of the cross are ambassadors of its message and of its power.

The Confusion of the cross

The Jews were looking for the Messiah, but they were looking for their Messiah, not God's. They had their preconceived ideas regarding the Messiah as to what he should look like, how he should communicate, what he should do, and who he should relate to. So when their religious leaders saw him embracing lepers and associating with prostitutes and with those who consorted with the nation's enemies they immediately rejected him. The fact is it did not matter what he said or did, for they rejected him because he did not fit with their concept of the Messiah.

But if they had a problem with his appearance and with those he identified as friends there was worse to come, because the cross would add to their confusion. Even the disciples were confused, because they also were Jews who looked for the Messiah. They had never considered that their journey in following Jesus would lead them to a place of Roman execution where they would watch from a distance as Christ was crucified. Jesus however sought to help them through their confusion by preparing them for his death and particularly for the cross.

He told the disciples in advance that he would be delivered up to die and also explained the manner of his death. On one occasion Peter, who suffered from a metaphoric form of foot and mouth disease, rebuked Jesus for speaking like this. But Jesus quickly corrected Peter and then made it clear that if anyone would come after him they must likewise take up the cross and follow him (see Matt. 16:21-24).

Even in following Jesus, Peter was still caught up with the whole Jewish thing regarding the concept of the Messiah. It is so easy to get caught up with the whole religious thing and to think that our calling is to defend God and to defend his word, and perhaps to throw a country in for good measure e.g. 'For God and Ulster' (Northern Ireland); for God and Ireland; for God and Israel; for God and America and so on. Such an attitude comes from a confused understanding of the cross, but its true ambassadors will always keep their focus.

Peter in his moments of confusion preferred the sword to the cross, but the sword represents what we think we can do, whereas the cross represents what God can do. What did not help Peter was the fact that he lived on the other side of the cross. He was part of the unfolding story as one of its main characters. Unlike us, Peter did not have the four Gospels at his disposal. He never saw the movies Ben Hur, the Greatest Story Ever Told, or the Passion of the Christ. He never heard Tony Compolo or his senior Pastor preach the classic message "It's Friday, but Sunday's coming". He did not know that beyond the cross there was a resurrection and an empty tomb.

Peter and the other disciples had never heard of Easter Sunday or of Good Friday. They never would have thought that that particular Friday, when Christ was crucified, would ever be called Good Friday and that they were destined to become central characters in the first ever Easter Sunday. On Friday they were confused, but when Sunday came the confusion was gone. On Friday Jesus was dead. His lifeless bloodied body was a pitiful sight as they removed it from the cross, but Sunday would tell a different story.

On Friday Mary the mother of Jesus was weeping bitterly, along with the other women and friends of Jesus, but Sunday would tell a different story. On Friday the skies were filled with darkness and the atmosphere was filled with despair, but Sunday was a brighter day. On Friday the disciples were like sheep without a shepherd; they felt leaderless, hopeless and helpless, but that was Friday. Sunday would once again tell a different story.

That particular Friday the hopes of many for a better world, both for themselves and their children, were dashed. But Sunday would tell a different story. On Friday it seemed that the forces of evil that had oppressed and suppressed the poor and the weak were very much in control, but Sunday would tell a different story. On Friday the demons of hell were premature in their celebrations, because Sunday would tell a different story. On Friday the religious Pharisees were claiming that the voice of Christ had been silenced and that the voice of religion was still the voice of God, but Sunday would tell a different story.

On Friday the lifeless bloodied body of Jesus was sealed inside the tomb by the use of a stone, but Sunday would tell a different story when the stone would be rolled away and the tomb would be empty. On Friday the disciples were truly confused, but on Sunday the light was switched on and someone was at home. The fact is without the resurrection of Christ even we would be confused. In fact Paul said that if Christ is not raised then there is no resurrection beyond the grave and therefore "we are to be pitied more than all men" (1 Cor. 15:19).

The Challenge of the cross

The cross might well be foolishness to some and a stumbling block to others, but to those who believe it is the power of God and therefore presents the greatest challenge ever to all men. Its message is so powerful that Paul was adamant when he said, "We preach Christ crucified; a stumbling block to Jews and foolishness to gentiles" (1 Cor. 1:23). The cross presents such a challenge because it is a place of self-sacrifice; a place of personal humility; and a place of total surrender. It truly is a life changing experience.

It is at the cross where true ambassadors of Christ are birthed. It is from the cross that true ambassadors of Christ go forward to represent him in a dark and dangerous world, loving not their lives even unto death and overcoming the works of the devil by the blood of the lamb and by the word of their testimony (see Rev. 12:11).

The challenge of the cross is not just in coming to it, but in going out from it. Jesus called us to take up the cross and follow him in the path of total surrender. He said, "If anyone would come after me, he must deny himself and take up his cross and follow me" (Matt. 16:24). He also said, "anyone who does not take his cross and follow me is not worthy of me" (Matt. 10:38).

Jesus is not meaning that we should all literally take up a wooden cross and carry it through the streets of our cities, but that we walk and live with the sacrificial sense of self denial.

However, some might feel the challenge to take up a literal cross and walk with it for specific reasons as I have done several times in my life. On two occasions it was a brief walk through the main road of my home community during two separate feuds that had broken out between rival terrorist organisations. The other occasion was a 40 Day Cross Walk when I carried a cross around the main roads of the Shankill and Falls communities in Belfast. These communities have been warring against each other for many years and are divided by a 20ft concrete wall that represents a deeper division in their hearts and minds. I have mentioned this wall several times in this book. The full story of this Cross Walk has been documented in my second book 'The Cross and the Gun'.

The purpose of this walk was to lift the cross above the physical, political, and spiritual walls of division. Everyday I received messages of encouragement and prayer support from across the world, including some from Arthur Blesset. However, one person wrote and said she felt as though she were carrying an invisible cross as she daily lived her life in obedience to Christ. The fact is every ambassador of Christ is an ambassador of the cross carrying with them daily an invisible cross, yet one that is seen in how they live and walk before men and before God.

The story of the cross truly is the greatest story ever told. This story can be revealed in word and can also be told in song, but the greatest method of communicating the story of the cross is in and through the surrendered lives of its ambassadors. We are told that Jesus "for the joy set before him endured the cross" (Heb. 12:2). If he did this for us, then he deserves that we also should take up our cross on his behalf and follow him.

The cross is calling out to a lost humanity as it beckons each person to come and bow down before it in true repentance and in total surrender. But the same cross cries out to its ambassadors and says "Don't Just Sit There". Many have heard this call down through the centuries, some before and some after Calvary. In responding to this call many of its ambassadors have become history makers. It is almost like the cross cried out to them as follows:

"Moses, don't just sit there in the backside of the desert, but get up and leave for Egypt. There are people in captivity who have waited a long time for this moment".

"Joshua, don't just sit there being content with playing second fiddle, but get up and take your place at the front, for Moses is dead and these people need someone who will finally get them across the Jordan and into Canaan".

"Gideon, don't just sit there looking after that wheat, but get up and get out there and take back those fields from the Midianites so that wheat can once again be harvested by a people who are free from oppression".

"Peter, don't just sit there feeling guilty about your denials and your swearing, but get up and get out there as one who is truly forgiven, for there are lambs and sheep that need feeding with the best you can give them".

"Thomas, don't just sit there trying to figure it all out, but get up and get out there and with full confidence take this message of the cross to the world for which Christ died".

"Paul, don't just sit there complaining about your little thorn, but get up and get on with it, for there are journeys to take, cities to visit, and churches to establish".

And hey, forgive me for saying so, but if Forrest Gump could get up and get out there and make something of his life, then surely so can we as ambassadors of Christ!

Get the point? Don't just sit there.

Jack McKee
www.newlifecitychurch.co.uk